P9-DWT-312

MONTANA 1864

Indians, Emigrants, and Gold in the Territorial Year

KEN EGAN JR.

RIVERBEND
PUBLISHING

Montana 1864: Indians, Emigrants, and Gold in the Territorial Year
Copyright © 2014 by Ken Egan Jr.

Published by Riverbend Publishing, Helena, Montana

ISBN 13: 978-1-60639-076-4

Printed in the United States of America.

1 2 3 4 5 6 7 8 9 0 SB 22 21 20 19 18 17 16 15 14

All rights reserved. No part of this book may be reproduced, stored, or transmitted in any form or by any means without the prior permission of the publisher, except for brief excerpts for reviews.

Cover and text design by Sarah Cauble, www.sarahcauble.com

Riverbend Publishing
P.O. Box 5833
Helena, MT 59604
1-866-787-2363
www.riverbendpublishing.com

Front cover photos
Top row, left to right: Granville Stuart, Mollie (Mary Ronan) and James Sheehan, John M. Bozeman, Plenty Coups, Jim Bridger
Middle row, left to right: Abraham Lincoln, Father De Smet, Calamity Jane, Montana gold panner (Montana Historical Society Research Center Photograph Archives, Helena)
Bottom row, left to right: Sitting Bull, Awbonnie Tookanka Stuart, Last Chance Gulch in Helena, General Alfred Sully
Front cover background: A hand-written record of the May 24, 1863, meeting of the Bannack Mining District. (Montana Historical Society Research Center Photograph Archives, Helena)

*This book is dedicated to
Humanities Montana/Montana Committee for the Humanities
Board and Staff Members, Current and Past,
With deepest appreciation for your commitment to bringing
Montanans together to learn and reflect on our past, present,
and future—you have made a profound, lasting difference to
the quality of life in our state*

ALSO BY KEN EGAN JR.

Hope and Dread in Montana Literature
The Riven Home: Narrative Rivalry in the American Renaissance
Writers Under the Rims: A Yellowstone County Anthology (co-editor)

CONTENTS

INTRODUCTION p. 9

VISIONS p. 17

JANUARY p. 23

In which the Hunkpapa Sioux weigh their options, Henry Plummer meets his fate, Mollie Sheehan suffers a fall from innocence, Gad Upson takes over as Blackfeet agent, and William Andrews Clark sows the seeds of a great fortune.

FEBRUARY p. 39

In which Nathaniel Langford meets with President Lincoln, Francis Thompson carries an important item to Washington City, and a ranching dynasty is born.

MARCH p. 49

In which James Stuart leads an expedition to the Big Horn, Johnny Grant's seven children are baptized, and Charlie Russell is born.

APRIL p. 69

In which John Owen lobbies for a new territory and spring comes for the Kootenai people.

MAY p. 83

In which James Vail tells the story of his failed mission at Sun River Indian Farm, the Salish gather the bitterroot and negotiate a treaty, and President Lincoln signs Montana Territory into existence.

JUNE p. 115

In which Abram Voorhees journeys to and from Montana and summer comes to the Assiniboine.

JULY p. 127

In which General Sully leads an attack on the Hunkpapa Sioux and their allies, street fights break out in Benton City on the Fourth of July, a Protestant minister arrives on the Madison River, and Last Chance Gulch is discovered.

AUGUST p. 147

In which the Crows defend their homeland against the Sioux and Cheyenne, James Fergus sends an angry letter to Pamelia, his wife, Bull Lodge becomes a great leader of the A'aninin, John Bozeman founds a town, and Victor Charlo describes home.

SEPTEMBER p. 175

In which Coth-co-co-na tells the story of her marriage to Malcolm Clarke, Gad Upson distributes annuities to the allied Blackfeet nations, and James Welch provides an overview of settlement.

OCTOBER p. 187

In which prospectors stampede Silver Bow Creek, the Chinese settle in German Gulch, the Republicans hold a rally in Virginia City, and Sisters of Providence establish a boarding school at St. Ignatius.

NOVEMBER p. 199

In which the Sand Creek Massacre is told, Sweet Medicine prophesies the Cheyenne future, and Higgins, Worden, and Pattee begin building Missoula Mills.

DECEMBER p. 207

In which Judge Hosmer calls out the Vigilantes, Governor Edgerton calls the first territorial legislature into session, and Calamity Jane arrives in Montana.

AFTER p. 221

In which Mollie Sheehan dances on news of Lincoln's death, Victor sends a letter of concern to Governor Edgerton, and M. L. Smoker offers a final wisdom.

ACKNOWLEDGMENTS p. 225

SOURCES p. 226

REFERENCES p. 236

INDEX p. 245

INTRODUCTION

MONTANA TURNS 150 YEARS OLD IN 2014, YET THE YEAR OF its founding, 1864, remains elusive, veiled in legend and half-formed thoughts. That creation story has been obscured by later, iconic events such as the Battle of the Little Bighorn, the transition of Indians to reservation life, the collapse of the open range, the rise of the Anaconda Copper Company, and the homestead boom of the early 20th century. In the rain-shadow of these grand historic peaks, which events from 1864 survive? Vigilantes, Virginia City, and the Bozeman Trail might come to mind, in large part because of vivid writing handed down to us from the early territorial days and through the talents of such gifted storytellers as Dorothy Johnson. But what else? The phrase "Last Chance Gulch" has taken on totemic power for locals, and so Montanans might remember that what is now Helena was born of a desperate final prospecting effort by the misnamed "Four Georgians." Montanans still talk about the strong Southern leanings of early emigrants—again, thanks to the vivid prose of charismatic historians such as Joseph Kinsey Howard and K. Ross Toole. And a name such as "Granville Stuart" can ring a bell, though contemporary Montanans would be hard-pressed to define his role or achievements.

But who else resided here—or just passed through? Was mining the only occupation for white emigrants? How did emigrants arrive in the region—and how did they interact with the native peoples who had claimed the place as home for hundreds of years? Were there treaties in place in 1864, and if so, who was charged with implementing their provisions, and what were the results of those efforts? Was there a U.S. military presence?

And most importantly, how does 1864 matter for 2014—what is the meaning, the impact, the importance of that founding year for contemporary Montanans? *Montana 1864* offers answers to these intriguing questions.

To begin to provide those answers, I return in memory to Chicago, 1964. The Montana Centennial Train was making a brief stop on its journey to the New York World's Fair. My grandmother insisted my sisters, brothers and I accompany her to see the grand spectacle. Grandmother was a Montana matriarch who had been stranded in a Chicago suburb with her son's family following Grandfather's sudden death. No doubt this trip into the Midwestern metropolis was a nostalgic journey for her and an attempt to inoculate her grandchildren against the dire influences of Chicago. My siblings and I were children of the suburbs, soaking in a new rock sound, Catholic dogma, and the ultra-mediated world of Chicago TV stations. Images of Tarzan, Lucy, Beaver, Jesus, the Beatles, and Stan Mikita blurred in our minds with the rolling prairies, denuded of trees, that defined our physical landscape.

So imagine those six children, ranging in age from six to thirteen, gazing in rapt horror at *After the Battle*, a garish, larger-than-life painting depicting the aftermath of "Custer's Last Stand" that dominated one of the Centennial display cars.

The youngest boy, seven years old, focused on a single image among the many scenes of mutilation: A self-satisfied warrior completes the scalping of a light-haired, bearded soldier. So that's how it's done, the boy thought, that's what it means to claim the trophy of a dead man, a dead American—a quick slip of the knife around the forehead, a tug, and a piece of glory. Yet the boy was surprised by the almost serene look on the soldier's slack face—the child felt the dead man's shame for him, the loss of honor, the meaning of defeat, the triumph of savagery. A kind of futile fury surged through him, caused small hands to tighten into fists, as though he could strike down the smug victor.

I was that boy.

The Montana Centennial Train was a spectacle with a purpose, a story, a myth. It was, in fact, an elaborate marketing ploy, promoting a vision of Montana as a cowboy and recreation paradise, open for business. The three packed display cars offered up memorabilia from the Battle of the Little Bighorn, rifles, belt buckles, $1 million worth of gold nuggets, saddles, spurs, wheat, barley, and Indian artifacts. Large murals painted on the side of the train depicted a historical sequence from the buffalo days to mining to ranching culture, featuring Custer, Calamity Jane, and Bill Cody. Passengers included 306 people and 75 horses, along with the wagons and stagecoaches for the parades that accompanied each tour stop. Those who journeyed with the train remembered "there's never been a scheme as grand—almost like Barnum and Bailey Circus or almost like Buffalo Bill" and it was "Montana's greatest publicity stunt....It showed the lore of the West." The boosters melded movie westerns with one of those railroad pamphlets from the early 20th century that had lured unsuspecting homesteaders to Montana's high, dry plains, including my grandmother, who claimed land in northeastern Montana in 1913.

I return to Chicago 1964, as we commemorate the 150th anniversary of Montana Territory in 2014, asking what kind of memorial train we might design today—which stories, artifacts and myths would occupy our display cars? *Montana 1864* offers a virtual sesquicentennial train, telling stories of the diverse peoples that spent time in the territory during the year of its founding. This narrative train will feature these themes:

The many tribal nations that claimed the region as their homeland—their life ways, their changing ways, and their responses to an explosion of emigrants spurred by gold;

The rush of men from North and South, carrying the Civil War in their minds and hearts, even as many of them flee the fight, and the physical and political battles that ensued in the just-created territory;

The revelation of many characters who have taken on near-mythic status yet remain obscure, the likes of Henry Plummer, Granville Stuart, John Bozeman, Jim Bridger, Malcolm Clarke, Victor, Plenty Coups, Pretty Shield, Crazy Horse, Sitting Bull, John Owen, William Andrews Clark, and Calamity Jane;

The stories of many less-known figures, just as revealing, who deserve more attention in our recollections, such as Mary Ronan, James and Martha Jane Vail, Pamelia Fergus, Bull Lodge, Coth-co-co-na, Jefferson Davis Doggett, and Alfred Sully;

The creation of towns so central to contemporary Montana: Bozeman, Helena, Missoula, and Butte;

The establishment of the very trails we still follow as we drive through this vast, beautiful space: the Corinne Road from Utah to Montana is now I-15; I-90 traces trails laid down by John Mullan and John Bozeman, not to mention much older tribal roads to the buffalo herds on the plains; the Hi-Line paves over a critical route for Piegan, Gros Ventre, Assiniboine, and other tribal hunters and warriors, as well as the Northern Overland Route blazed by Captain James Fisk;

The struggle over creating the Territory's first laws, a battle waged over such fundamental questions as whether African Americans would have the right to vote.

These stories carry their freight of meaning, their deep implications for our contemporary lives. Returning in memory to the year of Montana's founding, we realize that until the Civil War, what we now call Montana seemed remote, crudely mapped, and dangerous for most Americans. Indian nations—especially the Piegan, Gros Ventres, Sioux, and Northern Cheyenne—had defended the place well. It was a sustaining setting for Northern Plains peoples' life. This is not to say Indians lived in a state of nature—they made choices, their natural world was undergoing constant change, and intertribal violence was real and painful.

But the mountains and plains offered a life source, a ground for tribal nations, which was not to last.

It was only a matter of time before the imperialistic United States would figure out what to make of the place. In the aftermath of the fur trade that essentially ended in the 1850s, fewer than 1,000 whites lived in the region. Fur trappers and traders such as Alexander Culbertson, James Kipp, and Malcolm Clarke established their own sustainable lives by marrying native women and practicing accommodation balanced with tough-minded negotiation. Yet the nation as a whole remained indifferent to the headwaters of the Missouri, for as Daniel Webster opined,

> What do we want with this vast, worthless area, this region of savages and wild beasts?

Everything changed with gold. Once the metal was discovered in massive, accessible quantities in 1862, American uses for the region quickly multiplied: source of bullion to finance the Union cause; farming and ranching to support the gold boom; towns to support the empire for liberty. And of course, Montana became a safety valve, a place to start over for so many wounded in body and soul by the Civil War. This place became the occasion, the opportunity to recreate "America" according to each dreamer's personal and regional visions. No wonder the white population of the place surged from fewer than 1,000 to more than 20,000 within three years (historians estimate that 20,000 native people lived in the area now called Montana).

All of which starts to explain the volume and intensity of conflict unleashed by the gold boom. It was not just a contest for resources, though it was all of that too; it was also a conflict of life ways and fundamental, world-defining beliefs. It was a collision of nations. The individual human beings profiled in these pages often acted with a sense of historical destiny, historical inevitability. They saw their actions as part of an unfolding pattern of history, most often seen as divine or theological history, the realization of a grand plan. In this way, personal ambition aligned with national destiny, giving even the most venal actions the allure of fate.

Montana in 1864 was more than the site of a contest of personal wills or even specific national goals—it became a battleground over the sense of a nation, of an incorporated people, of the right to claim and inhabit the land as fully authentic human beings. It became a struggle over the very meaning of what constitutes a people.

These stories will be told month-by-month, giving the contemporary reader a chance to experience how events unfolded in time in that founding year. My hope is that readers will feel the flow of time, the role of chance, the surprise of seeing a familiar character in a new light. This book can be read as a braided narrative in which historical figures appear and reappear, taking on new dimensions, unexpected angles. For example, Henry Plummer's death is narrated in January, but his full story does not emerge until James Vail tells his woeful tale in May; we first meet Mollie Sheehan in January 1864 as she encounters a horrific death—then meet her again in March when hearing Granville Stuart's story, and again in "After" when witnessing her reaction to Abraham Lincoln's assassination; Gad Upson, a notoriously ill-informed agent to the Blackfeet and Gros Ventre nations, weaves through the months, distributing annuities and ill feelings in equal doses; Jim Bridger emerges for the first time in April with John Owen's account of his return journey to Montana, but he will make an appearance at later points, such as Abram Voorhees' memorable view of him in June and his affiliation with John Bozeman as described in August. Readers can use the Table of Contents and the Index as means to track various characters through the months.

To present the tales of these diverse peoples, at times the narrative shifts perspective, enters new voices. While most of the stories are told from the point of view of a contemporary historian looking back and interpreting events, on several occasions tales are narrated in alternative voices. In May, for example, James Vail tells the story of his family's move to the Sun River Indian Farm two years previously, their meeting with Henry Plummer, his sister-in-law's marriage to Plummer, and the disaster that followed in early 1864. Given the richness of the tale, it made sense to allow James, a witness to all the events and a human being deeply implicated in the action, to render his account. In August, a major battle between the Crows and the allied Sioux, Cheyenne, and Arapaho is presented from multiple points of view, those of two Crow witnesses, Pretty Shield and Plenty Coups, and that of a major Lakota history. To indicate that the event is being told word-for-word by these witnesses, those sections are presented in block quotations. I follow the same practice when narrating one of the most horrific events of all, the Sand Creek Massacre, in November.

My virtual Sesquicentennial Train offers a very different spectacle from the Montana Centennial Train I visited in 1964. It is the grandchild's privilege to rewrite the works of the elders. I trust that in another fifty years, on the 200th anniversary of Montana Territory, a new generation will reread the past in a way that makes sense to their lives, to their way of seeing Montana, and they will revise the Montana script yet again. No doubt young children will have their shocking encounters with images out of the past.

VISIONS

My son, you have now finished with the experiences that were allotted to you. You have made it clear to us that you are sincere in your ambition to become a great man. All of the important things which go to help one become famous have been given to you. Now that your wish is granted and your work done, you are to wait until you are told to begin exercising the powers that are given to you. Go now and prepare yourself, my son. As it was told you, you must get ready for the life you are to live.

SEVENTH VISION OF BULL LODGE, GROS VENTRE LEADER,
NEAR SWEET GRASS HILLS, CA. 1825

The general condition of the Indians of the Blackfeet nation, taken in the light of civilization, is degrading in the extreme; the first glimpses of Christianity or morality have not yet shed their benignant rays around them; their customs and habits are to-day the same as a quarter of a century ago. All the benefits they have received from their intercourse with the whites have tended rather to degrade than enlighten them. Their immoralities and vices are quickly discovered, and as easily followed; thus they have all the low vices of the whites added to their own degraded natures. The mantle of virtue, if it ever covered any of the whites that have lived in this country, certainly has not descended to the Indian; he yet stands a monument of savage royalty among his native mountains and prairies, free and untrammeled from the shackles of an enlightened conscience, or the virtuous examples of his white brethren, proud, haughty, and contented in the glorious exploits of his fathers, which he desires to emulate and, if possible, eclipse. To bring them out of this pit of degradation is the work of time.

GAD E. UPSON, BLACKFEET INDIAN AGENT, 1864

Every man for his principles—hurrah for Jeff Davis! let her rip.

BOONE HELM, JUST BEFORE HE IS HANGED BY VIGILANTES
AT VIRGINIA CITY, JANUARY 14, 1864

I came to what is now our magnificent state of Montana when it was a trackless wilderness, the only white inhabitants being Jesuit fathers, and a few Indian traders and trappers at the missions and trading posts; when the mountains and valleys were the homes of countless herds of buffalo, elk, deer, moose, antelope, bear, and mountain sheep; when the streams swarmed with fish and beaver and the Indians were rich and respectable. I have watched the frontier push from the Mississippi river to the Rocky mountains, there to join hands with the settlements that had advanced from the Pacific coast; and from the Rio Grande to the Yellowstone, there to greet civilization that moved from Hudson Bay. I saw in the valley of the Yellowstone the last of the buffalo, the last of the wild free Indians, the last of "The Great West that Was."

GRANVILLE STUART, EARLY EMIGRANT, CA. 1918

I'm sitting here in this very old tribal world.

JULIE CAJUNE, SALISH EDUCATOR, 2009

JANUARY

In which the Hunkpapa Sioux weigh their options, Henry Plummer meets his fate, Mollie Sheehan suffers a fall from innocence, Gad Upson takes over as Blackfeet agent, and William Andrews Clark sows the seeds of a great fortune.

All of the months of the year had names. Rightfully, it was each moon that had a name. Beginning with the month of January, the [Blackfeet] call it the Moon of Big Smoke, the Moon That Helps Eat. That's because in January, when the air is very still, the smoke from the tipis go straight upward, and for some reason it comes very big in size from the tipi. "Helps eat" is because the weather is so cold, no one could get out to do anything outside, everyone just about has to stay inside of the tipi. When one is always near the food, it's always tempting to eat, and naturally the food goes faster.
So January is the Help Eat Moon.

I T IS BITTER CHILL IN THE CAMPS AT THE CONFLUENCE OF the Powder and Yellowstone rivers. Hunkpapa Sioux and their Santee guests have gathered to conserve their energies and talk defense of the homeland. The wasichu have begun to invade the sacred lands, the source of vision, sustenance, and memory. The Americans, so restless and unaware of the past, do not respect the place of the fathers and mothers, the place of the creator and all his creation.

Battles in Minnesota during 1862, culminating with the mass hanging of thirty-eight Santee Sioux, the largest public execution in United States history (and the most inglorious death that the Sioux can imagine), have driven the Sioux farther west, closer to their hated Crow enemies. A campaign by the U.S. military in Dakota Territory just last summer, clumsy and ineffective as it seemed, reinforced belief in this winter camp that a final war is upon them—these invaders will not relent, they will not be persuaded, even when outmaneuvered, disoriented, and humiliated. There is something fiercely foolish and unyielding about these light-skinned, hairy wanderers. They seem lost, and lost animals strike out in blind fury.

It was not supposed to come to this. The Fort Laramie Treaty of 1851, completed just a few years earlier, held promise of grudging respect and accommodation. Tribal nations had been assured hunting ranges, annuities, and, above all, the chance to be left alone. While the signatories could hardly be expected to abide by the strict boundaries on where they could hunt, camp, and fight, they could be counted on to leave emigrants to their own devices, as long as those wanderers did not encroach upon the cherished buffalo ranges and sacred places.

Fortunately, something in the American eye misses the wonder of the Powder River, flowing north into the mightier Yellowstone River through a vast, open valley, the massive Big Horn Mountains rising to the west, the profound Black Hills to the east. Where these people see abundance and life, especially the great bison herds, the Americans see desert, a bleak scene, a blank. Maybe it is the *wasichus'* obsession with raising wheat and running their "white horns"—the Powder River is not made for that way of living. Maybe it is because the whites' eyes are focused so tightly on lands to the west, lands beyond these plains and mountains, rumored to be green year-round and ideal for the farmer and rancher.

Yet even there the people at the confluence of two rivers have reason to wonder and to fear. What is this need for land that causes so many families to risk everything on a painful, often futile path? What agencies, what energies propel them to pack creaking wagons and follow lumbering oxen to seek some elusive, unlikely home beyond the great mountain ranges? There must be something truly horrific in the world to the east to cause so much uprooting, rage, and desperation. All that tramping and camping and foolishness had split the great bison herd, depleted their range, diminished their numbers. It had also brought disease to the people.

And now gold, that slippery metal, calls many more to the headwaters of the Missouri, country long protected by remoteness and the determined resistance of the native people. The nations had welcomed trade for skins, exchanges yielding metal pots, guns, tobacco, coffee, sugar, and yes, whiskey. But that was a simple, clear transaction, stable and knowable. Of course there was cheating and misleading and hard feelings on both sides, but how the nations had come to love the trade goods that made their lives on the often-harsh plains easier, better. A few forts, isolated and unassuming, did no harm, they seemed so flimsy and temporary. Men like Alexander Culbertson and Malcolm Clarke married Blackfeet women and lived close to the many tribes that would trade beaver and buffalo and wolf skins for manufactured goods.

But now, this is a new kind of American invader, no pretending to seeking home or permanence, just a mad dash to grab the metal and return east to acquire and ascend. These new emigrants have that remorseless glint in the eye, that perfervid gaze that announces they will give no quarter, not back down. It must be the last chance for many of these drifting men, few women or children to soften their consciences, their language, or their gestures. Foolish men, who should know better when they encounter the scattered remains of their countrymen, destroyed by chance meetings with resentful young men from the allied tribes, and from the enemies too, those Piegan and Crows. And they come from every direction—from south along the Powder River, from east out of Santee country, and up the Missouri River in those infernal boats powered by monstrous vapors.

So now is the time to fight, now is the time to signal no more ground given, no more free passage, no more averting the eyes to assure that the annuities, often paltry and inedible, will be delivered. No more pretending that this violation of land and people is temporary, fragile, and futile. The people will strike against the invaders. Spring cannot come too soon.

HENRY PLUMMER RECLINES ON HIS BED, ILL-DISPOSED ON THIS bitterly cold January day in Bannack City. Yet for all his discomfort, he remains a handsome man to the end. It is those looks, those manners, those delicate gestures and calm smile that have carried him to this moment.

The sound of boots and muted voices startle in the cold air of noon on Grasshopper Creek. His sister-in-law, Mrs. Vail, glances at him with alarm, and he rises up halfway with a premonition. It has come at last.

Dark-coated, bearded men, familiar to him from his time as sheriff of Bannack, surge into the cabin and promptly bind his hands. They seem remorseless, determined, imperturbable. Yet as the fifty men force-march him toward an end foreseen, he calls out for Wilbur Sanders, whose cabin is nearby, to intervene.

Sanders, nephew of Sidney Edgerton, judge in Idaho Territory, is a lawyer and a Republican, and damned proud of both. He and Plummer had shared Thanksgiving dinner just a few weeks before and seemed on the best of terms.

What the handsome man cannot know is that Sanders is the very engine of this vigilante mob, the source of will and reason that compels them to end the life of a man many still like and respect.

Bannack, Montana, in the 1860s. Montana Historical Society Research Center Photograph Archives, Helena, Montana

And so Sanders says to the condemned man in a voice without inflection, without emotion, "It is useless for you to beg for your life. [T]he affair is settled and cannot be altered. You are to be hanged. You cannot feel harder about it than I do, but I cannot help it if I could."

Plummer knows now that there is little chance of eluding this end. He glances at the two men who join him at this moment of terror, Buck Stinson and Ned Ray, and pity surges through him. When Red Yeager and George Brown were strung up just six days earlier, he knew this possibility loomed. Yet through all these years of moving and loving and killing and explaining, he never thought he'd see the end of a rope. That's why he always went armed—knife and pistol on his person, even as he slept—so he would never have to meet this moment. How ironic, then, that on this very day he would have set his weapons aside to sleep off some obscure ailment. He'd been caught unawares.

In truth, he has been ineffectual of late, distracted and slow to realize what was happening. Maybe it is sheer exhaustion from years of planning and concealing, of threatening and executing, and then finding a reason or leaving altogether. This dead-end mining town in the eastern hinterlands of Idaho Territory seems as good a place as any to bring that career to an end. Only he wishes his right wrist worked properly, having been destroyed by a bullet in a shoot-out just last year with a sworn enemy who managed to escape, and now pulsing and painful when bound behind him. He suspects that malformed wrist has given him away during the hold-ups, his awkward way of handling the gun the "tell" that provides proof of his guilt.

Would his wife, departed for Iowa after living with him for a short time in Bannack, remember him, mourn him? They had met by sheer chance at the government Indian farm on Sun River. What a sweet girl, Electa, so alone there in that ramshackle farm on a river flowing out of the mighty Rocky Mountains just to the west, the river lit up by the golden glow of sunset on summer evenings. If only he could go back now, recover that time. They married just last June, but he had sent her back home in September because he sensed the danger, not just of these self-righteous, hard men, but of men out of his past who arrived in Bannack City unbidden, like demons or ghouls, calling forth his past deeds. No, he did not want Electa to hear those things, or face a day like this. In this moment of death, he is proud and grateful he has spared his young bride this horror.

Yet he pleads for his life, seeing some hesitation, some doubt in his executioners' tight faces. He proclaims his innocence, tells them he has done nothing wrong and deserves a fair trial. No break in their determination. And so he asks simply that he be allowed to put his affairs in order, to speak with his sister-in-law, have a chance to send final word to his dear wife.

They will not relent. The Vigilance Committee knows that in the past, such delays in meting out gold camp justice have led to freedom for the condemned. No, a decision was made with tense deliberation the night before, and there's no backing down now. The very man elected to protect the peace has been the ringleader of a pack of road agents who have murdered and stolen and lied. No more lies, no more chances.

And now the handsome man loses his composure, pleading for his life, imploring that they let him see his wife one final time. His fear only increases with the rushing arrival of Joseph Swift, a gentle young man who had befriended Plummer during their time together at Sun River Farm. Joseph weeps, implores, trembles and gestures. One of the hard men drags Joseph out of the inner circle of doom, but his wailing can be heard over the din.

The horror rises further with the raging curses of Ned Ray, his mistress weeping just out of view, the grim truth of death, his living and breathing about to be extinguished.

Ned dies ugly—he puts his hand up through the noose as he is dropped, and so his neck is not broken on the instant. He strangles in the air.

Stinson offers to confess as he's about to be strung up, but the handsome man stops him with the words, "We've done enough already to send us all to hell." Stinson is luckier than Ned—he gets a clean drop.

The handsome man makes one final plea—he'll leave the country, they'll never see him again.

The vigilantes, many of whom know the condemned man well, repeat that it's all over. They place the noose around his neck. He gets a clean drop.

Henry Plummer is dead.

SHE HAS BRIGHT EYES AND A QUICK MIND. MOLLIE SHEEHAN, eleven years old, moves with childish confidence through the mad world of Virginia City. She sees the greed, and the hard work, and the exhaustion, and the hurdy-gurdy houses, and the casual fist-blows and shots. The buildings are ramshackle and unstable, made to last only the time it takes to make a killing and head back to the States. She also sees the extraordinary profusion of flowers in this remote mountain town, and bears witness to the shifts of light and cloud across the mountain faces, and listens for the almost shocking fecundity of bird songs.

Mollie sees and knows in part because she's the proud daughter of an ambitious but unlucky man. Her father, James, an energetic Irishman seeking the main chance on the undefined terrain of Idaho Territory, has tried and failed to make a living as freighter for the gold mines in Colorado, and now he's brought his growing family to this even more remote and wide-open town, born just the summer before, springing to life from Alder Gulch as if by magic, the very emblem of the land of gold.

James's is the familiar story of the 19th-century immigrant on the make, pursuing that elusive thing called opportunity

Mollie Sheehan (Mary Ronan) with her father, James. MANSFIELD LI-
BRARY ARCHIVES AND SPECIAL COLLECTIONS, MISSOULA, MONTANA

across the vast continent. He embodies all the contradictions of his adopted country's beliefs, loving the chance to begin anew time and again, yet he's a Democrat to the core, true to his Irish lineage, a staunch supporter of the working man and distrustful of all that Republican sentimentality about the coloreds. He's lived enough, struggled enough, to know that pain and disappointment are allotted equally to mankind, and "slave" is a relative condition. He resents the violence of the Union war against the Confederacy, even as he loves the United States with an almost religious mania that defies all those Know Nothings who assume an Irishman places the Church above all else. No, he would give his life for his new country, but given his young family, he needs to find the means to support them. And so he runs freight to this chaotic town, following the Mullan Road from Fort Benton and the Corinne Road from Salt Lake City. James is no fool, for all the need to risk life and limb to freight supplies over the expansive land through Blackfeet and Bannock country. He knows desperados prey on the unsuspecting, striking as if by secret knowledge.

Besides this understanding of the risks of his work, James knows he has a rare thing in young Mary, affectionately known as Mollie. There's some easy, silent rapport between father and daughter, an occult understanding. He has come to count on her precocious intelligence and apparent wisdom. She is the daughter of his first, much-mourned wife, a spark of that love and a gem of unusual brilliance.

As for Mollie, Virginia City proves a varied playground for her mind and imagination. She feels all the heartache and desire of these young men, cut loose from their families and so alone. They come from all over America and the world, the accents giving away homes north, south, and foreign. She has fallen half in love with some of them, especially Jack Gallagher, tall and gallant, a fine storyteller who accompanied her family on their journey north to Bannack just the summer before, praising

Mollie for her vivid memory of Little Eva's dying in *Uncle Tom's Cabin*, a tale she loved repeating by rote around the campfire.

Today holds a special horror, then. As bright-eyed Mollie walks home from school, she is startled by the sight of five figures hanging from a roof beam, and two of those dead men are familiar to her: Clubfoot George, who had treated her kindly, and her own Jack Gallagher.

The world shifts in that moment, takes on new shadows and shades. How could the people of Virginia City, even in their exhaustion, frenzy, and venality, murder these men? What forces operate beneath the surface of life to make such a thing possible? What had precocious Mollie missed about Jack, the charming man who seemed so kind, so gentlemanly?

In time Mollie will come to know the stories of the vigilantes and the road agents, partly through the words of her teacher, Thomas Dimsdale, printed in the *Montana Post* newspaper. She already knows of the murder of men in lonely places on the dark trails leading from Virginia City, the growing fear as this fifteen-mile string of towns along Alder Gulch yield as much gold as any strike in the west, including California and Colorado, giving the desperados ample opportunity to practice their wicked trade. In time, Mollie will come to realize the vigilantes may have saved her father's life. Yet that image of Jack Gallagher hanging in silhouette will remain photographed in her mind the rest of her days. It will remind her of what a fallen, mysterious, sad world this can be.

THOUGH HE HOLDS THEM DEGRADED SAVAGES, IRREDEEMABLE, Gad Upson of Fort Benton knows it is his business to bring the Indians to peace so that emigrants can travel safely to the mines, the farms, and the new towns. These are the very places he witnessed coming north from Utah to assume his responsibilities— Bannack and Virginia City, the promising valley of the Madison

River, and the journey along the Missouri River that led to his new post.

The Piegan chiefs arrive today, the fifteenth day of the first month of the new year, less than one month after Upson's beginning as government representative at the Blackfoot Agency. They must commit to peace with the Gros Ventres, bring an end to war parties and raids that have afflicted the region before his coming.

In Upson's eyes, this is a godforsaken place, Fort Benton, just an aging adobe fort and a set of tumbledown buildings fronting the river, a place for steamboats to unload people and goods and then descend the Missouri. Nothing much stays here for long, certainly not in the bleak winter as the winds blow blinding snow and the mountains to the west rarely emerge from the cold fog.

Nonetheless, Upson is a man of duty and will do his best to enforce the provisions of the Blackfeet Treaty, struck in 1855 by Governor Isaac Stevens, granting annuities to the Piegans, Blood, Blackfeet, and Gros Ventres in return for their allowing safe passage to emigrants and attention to the Sun River Indian Farm, where Indians can redeem themselves by engaging in agriculture and leaving behind the barbarism of the hunt and battle. He holds in mind his predecessor Mr. Reed's observation that the Indians fear the flow of emigrants "lest there might be some design of getting their lands from them, which they could not consent to, as this had been their home as well as that of their fathers, and they hoped to make it the place of their graves and the home of their children."

The chiefs arrive without the paint on themselves or their horses that indicates martial intentions. To Upson, these inscrutable beings seem serious and sober, a very good thing, given the savages' fondness for whiskey. They must be weary of raiding to and fro with the Gros Ventres, and eager to receive again the food and supplies assured by the Americans' agreement with them.

They promise to send tobacco to the Gros Ventre chiefs to signal their desire for a meeting soon, but they inform Upson they cannot always control their young men, impulsive and eager for war honors.

Yet, he thinks, "There is no one thing that would prove more beneficial to these Indians than the presence of troops stationed for a time at this place; its effects would be electrical. It would strike terror into their midst, show them the power of the government, and arrest their depredations in horse-stealing."

WILLIAM ANDREWS CLARK, A SHARP YOUNG MAN ON THE MAKE, freighting goods from Salt Lake City to the Montana mines, purchases the following items from Francis Thompson, merchant, Bannack City:

2 boxes of butter 299 lbs.	*$299.00*
3 sacks of flour 261 lbs.	*208.80*
5 sacks of peaches 201 lbs.	*160.80*
1 box of 120 eggs doz.	*120.00*
129 lbs. of oats	*24.27*
Total	*$812.87*

From such humble beginnings are great fortunes made. Clark will become a "Copper King," wealthy beyond belief. His rise from a modest farming family in Pennsylvania is spectacular: He pockets a tidy $2,000 from his placer mining near Bannack, runs a successful freighting business to the newly born Montana towns, turns to banking to build his fortune, and caps his rise by purchasing four soon-to-be ultrarich mines in Butte: The Original, Colusa, Mountain Chief, and Gambetta. He summarizes his philosophy of living in this journal entry: "There was no lack of opportunities for those who were on the alert for making money." But seizing these opportunities would take tremendous hard work, beginning with his sluicing gold near Bannack: "To mine their dry Jeff Davis Gulch, W.A. and his pals had to strip off about four feet of the dirt and rock with picks and shovels to reach gold-infused loose sediment near the bedrock. Then they had to haul the sediment half a mile in a cart they had built from the front wheels of their Schuttler wagon. The water of nearby Colorado Creek ran through their handmade sluice boxes, the tiered channels creating eddies that allowed the heavier gold nuggets and gold dust to separate from the dirt and rock, or tailings."

Despite the enormous wealth earned in Montana, Clark will choose to end his days in the East, with a mansion in New York City, and a will sending his world-class art collection to the Corcoran Gallery in Washington, D.C. But not before he turns to the task of buying a U.S. Senate seat, giving him the privilege of being skewered by the nation's greatest humorist, one Mark Twain: "[H]e is as rotten a human being as can be found anywhere under the flag; he is a shame to the American nation, and no one has helped to send him to the Senate who did not know that his proper place was the penitentiary, with a chain and ball on his legs. To my mind he is the most disgusting creature that the republic has produced since Tweed's time."

William Andrews Clark, 1898. Photograph by Wilhelm, New York, New York. Montana Historical Society Research Center Photograph Archives, Helena, Montana

FEBRUARY

In which Nathaniel Langford meets with President Lincoln, Francis Thompson carries an important item to Washington City, and a ranching dynasty is born.

February is the Moon of the Eagle, when the eagle returns from the winter migration. Also it is known as the Hatching Time of the Owl. The owl takes time to grow, he is awful slow. So to be ready for the spring months and able to fly, the owl hatches in February. This is true for other predatory animals or birds. The owl must be able to fly when all of the summer birds and hibernating animals come out for the warmer months. February is also the moon of the dreaded northern blizzard. The [Blackfeet] call it Taking Orderly Position for the Attack.

N ATHANIEL LANGFORD, PIONEER, SITS BESIDE PRESIDENT Abraham Lincoln on this gray day in squalid Washington City. He has traveled the hard road from Idaho Territory to the riven nation's capital to lobby for a new territory, one that would bring government to the wide open, dangerous country he has come to covet, and yes, to make sure that government is built on true American principles. Langford, like other key lobbyists Sidney Edgerton and Francis Thompson, takes himself and his cause very seriously. They are creating a reborn, rechristened United States, described so vividly by this very president in an address delivered just last November at Gettysburg in a ceremony dedicating the cemetery honoring those killed in that horrendous battle. "A new birth of freedom" has become the chorus of Republican souls. And toward that higher goal, the headwaters of the Missouri must be made into a new territory, for as Langford wrote to Minnesota Congressman Ignatius Donnelly recently, the region's gold mines "may be made to yield annualy [sic] sufficient to pay the interest on a national war debt of 2,000,000,000," if the gold can be procured with all due efficiency and speed.

Langford had arrived in the region in 1862 with Captain Fisk's Northern Overland Expedition, the first such effort to bring emigrants to the gold camps of the northern Rockies from the upper Midwest by way of Dakota Territory. These emigrants are the vanguard in establishing the path from St. Paul to Fort Benton, the harbingers of the railroad that will ultimately settle the region's fate. It is no coincidence that these Argonauts are overwhelmingly sympathetic to the Union cause—federal officials want to assure the secessionists and their sympathizers do not dominate a region likely to become a full-blown territory.

An ambitious, energetic, commanding man, Langford was born in New York but took his talents to Minnesota when he and the state were young, determined to grow up with the country. His forays into civilization- and business-building will provide the template, the experience, to succeed in the not-yet-created Montana. His businesses faltering, the War of the Rebellion exploding, he chose the path to opportunity by becoming third in command of Fisk's party. By Langford's account, it was a dangerous, fraught journey through country dominated by hostile natives, particularly the Sioux and Blackfeet, and he gave little quarter or respect to these peoples. They would always remain specters and barbarians in his eyes. Yet the Northern Overland Expedition passed without challenge from the dreaded natives.

Arriving in the vicinity of present-day Helena, Langford chose to stop for the winter rather than risk all by crossing the

Nathaniel P. Langford. NATIONAL PARK SERVICE

mountains in autumn. Like others who will emerge in these pages, the wanderer has arrived quite by accident in his land of promise. He cannot know that Grasshopper Creek—Bannack City—had been discovered just two months earlier. The Salmon River mines no longer offer the most promise—opportunity is suddenly near to hand. Langford was the man to seize it. He will set about projecting and scheming—by no means a term of derision or moral censure in these times—seeking the main chance for wealth and status. Among his many enterprises will be a bold effort to control the traffic and tolls on what would soon be called the Bozeman Trail.

LANGFORD, CASUALLY CALLED "TAN" BY FAMILY AND acquaintances, has arrived in Washington City with a clear purpose in mind, then. The boom towns east of the Bitterroot Mountains demand governance if they are to flourish economically and culturally, and so a new political entity must be carved out of Idaho Territory. Of course, Langford anticipates he will benefit monetarily and politically from this arrangement, but there's nothing immoral or double-faced about that. Before his hard work is done, he will serve as a delegate for President Lincoln at the convention nominating the latter for a second term as chief executive of the United States, and he will be named Collector of Revenues for the new territory, a role that positions him perfectly to understand the sources of wealth in a fresh country. In 1870, he will lead the first organized expedition to survey what will become Yellowstone National Park, and in time he will become that park's first superintendent.

But today Langford's conversation with President Lincoln seems a digression from his primary mission to help create a new territory. Instead, Langford broaches the topic of Mormon conduct in Utah, an issue raised by the emigrant's brief time in Salt Lake City during his journey east. Many "gentiles," or non-Mormons, had complained to him of their ill treatment at the hands of the Mormons, and their shocked discovery that Mormons practice plural marriage.

In Langford's mind, the Latter-Day Saints represent yet another threat to his vision of a free and equal nation. They are building a theocracy founded on a false religion, their fanaticism inspired by the delusions of Joseph Smith. They stand for disloyalty and disunion in another guise, not the loathsome religion of the slaveholders, it is true, but a wholly alien vision of utopia at the Great Salt Lake, a country apart, resistant to the Christian, democratic principles of America's founders.

Filled with his own righteous rage, and fearful this fanaticism might migrate north and infect his coming country, for he had heard an earful of these beliefs from passengers and coach drivers on the Corinne Road, Langford approaches the White House on this bleak day, and he has the good fortune to meet one of Lincoln's secretaries, Reverend E. D. Neill, another native of St. Paul, and so is granted an interview with President Lincoln. Langford finds the president pensive, somber. He listens carefully to Langford's appeal, leaning forward and staring at the floor, then observes that with the War of the Rebellion raging, he cannot direct men or money to the far west, and so must demur on the subject of the emerging Mormon empire. As is his wont, his charm, he makes his point by way of a story:

> I am like the old farmer out in Illinois. He and his boy
> had been grubbing the stumps, and clearing out the bushes from a large field before putting in the spring crop, and
> all the stumps had been cleared out except one—a large
> one with spreading roots, in which was a large hornet's
> nest, so that they could have a clear field for the plow—
> but the old man said it was getting late in the season and
> that it was time to get the seed into the ground. "Boys,"
> said he, "that stump and hornet's nest ought to come out,
> but we have so much other work on hand that we'll have

to plow around it this year." . . . So it is with me. That Utah hornet's nest ought to be rooted out—but there is more important work on hand just now, and we'll have to plow around it this year.

On February 22, Francis Thompson leaves Bannack on his own journey to Washington City. It proves arduous winter travel, requiring him to swim icy rivers, endure the threat of Indian attack on an emigrant trail, and carry a concealed pistol to protect his precious cargo, the gold needed to impress upon Congress the necessity of carving out a new political entity. Thompson is willing to bear this burden because, like Langford, he is driven by a cause, a belief, a hope. These founders of the soon-to-be Montana Territory perceive that self-interest not only aligns with national interest, but advances that larger purpose, enacts it, brings it into being. The bearded men so intent on creating a new territory for the headwaters of the Missouri River know, in their bones, that only by extending American institutions—executive, legislative, and judicial—to the wild lands can order, decency, and profit be brought to that distant place. They do not shy away from nor apologize for their quest for wealth—it is ever the way of the American, it is the very secret of the young nation's success. Men advance the nation by pursuing personal success, their seemingly isolated actions feeding the stream of democracy and prosperity. It is foolish to deny this equation. That folly lies at the heart of the Southern apostasy, for the "seceshes" hold that an aristocracy of birth and wealth should rule the lives of women, children, and slaves. They deny the value and higher purpose of free labor. They are blind to how a man becomes fully a citizen and a man through his own efforts, his independence, and his recognition of others' right to pursue the same course of self-culture, self-improvement. Self is nation.

Thompson had first reached Fort Benton in 1862 onboard the *Emilie*, one of the first steamers to dock at the world's innermost river port. He was accompanied by business partners intent on building a merchant empire in the Gold Creek region of Deer Lodge Valley, a group ambitiously called the American Exploring and Mineral Company. It seemed a simple enough proposition: Ferry goods up the Missouri from their home base in St. Louis for sale at exorbitant prices in the gold camps of the remote Rockies. The scheme depended on several dominoes falling into place, however, including a reliably high water level on the Missouri (far from a sure thing), the continued influx of prospectors (a likely thing), and the failure of competition (an unknown thing). A child of Massachusetts, Thompson arrived at this time and place after a successful law career in the upper Midwest, the very source of connections and funds that will serve the lobbying cause in Washington City so well. He was attracted to opportunity on the upper Missouri by American restlessness (what is a man if he is not on the make?) and a desire for better health, promised by the dry, clean air of the high plains and northern Rockies. His one and only exposure to an actual battle during the War of the Rebellion also encouraged him to abscond from that conflict. Thompson's merchant empire would never materialize, and he would return east to make a tidy profit promoting investment opportunities in Montana Territory, but he would also leave behind one of the very best sources on those early years of the new territory, his well-written, detailed, often very funny journal.

That journal records that on his bitter trek to the nation's capital in 1864, Thompson carries a special specimen of gold, one that will prove essential to bringing the new territory into being:

> It happened that a few days before starting, in retorting a lot of gold which had been gathered by quicksilver, over a blacksmith's fire, that the crucible broke and the

gold ran down into the cinders, making when congealed, a most beautiful spangle of the value of $1,500. This wonderful specimen Col. Hunkins purchased of me and requested that after I had exhibited it at Washington and at my home in Massachusetts, that I should send it to his daughter in Galena, Ill., for her to use as a mantel ornament.

Thompson also carries political influence, and that is the more effective currency in this campaign to create a new territory by dividing Idaho. The founders had agreed to this scheme shortly after Edgerton's arrival in Bannack, but they had waited to execute it until the road agent threat had been eliminated. Each in his own way would hold sway with his representatives and senators, and so each would spend a month or two or three in Washington City making personal appeals to their members of Congress:

Being with Judge Edgerton, admitted to the floor of the House, we, or at least our gold nugget, became the center of attraction to scores of the members and officials of the House, and several senators came over to see the remarkable specimen, which all thought was as nature had made it. We improved our opportunity to impress upon the members the necessity of the immediate organization of the new Territory. I was much aided by Hon. William B. Washburn, member from my home district in Massachusetts, and Mr. [Charles] Upson from Michigan, a valued friend.

FEBRUARY IS CALVING-OUT SEASON, THE TIME OF HARDEST work for sheep and cattle ranchers as they struggle day and night to make sure their livestock are born healthy and survive the wet, chilly conditions. The calves must wean by fall so they can fatten up over the winter.

One of Montana's foremost ranchers, Jefferson Davis Doggett, has just been born in Virginia City on Halloween day, 1863. He may be the first American born in the new town, though his name hints at divided loyalties on the question of the nation's future. His family has deep roots in the South: His grandfather, James, a scion of Virginia, had worked as a plantation overseer in Kentucky, where he married and produced a son, Moses. Yet, like so many Americans in the pre-Civil War years, this Southern family chose chance and opportunity over fealty to their home ground, emigrating first to Indiana, then Iowa, then Colorado. Moses will make the move to Montana the summer of '63, and so a Montana ranching legacy is born.

Moses joins the migration onward to Helena in 1864, where he continues to mine for a time, and then determines that "mine the miners" is a fine philosophy: it is better (and far more sustainable) to provide food for the stampeders rather than count on the stroke of luck, the strike of chance. And so, after a brief stay in Helena, he establishes a homestead on the Missouri River near present-day Townsend, the place he will ranch until his death in 1895.

His son Jeff will pursue adventures of his own over the first thirty years of his life, joining the stampede to Coeur d'Alene in 1884, running packs from Thompson Falls to Idaho, and then settling down in the Smith River Valley. He will ultimately purchase a ranch on Duck Creek, northeast of Townsend and ideal for extensive sheep ranching. He will also help found a bank, one of those foundational institutions that lubricate the local economy and assure capital for ranchers and farmers. Despite his family's deep roots in the Old South, Jeff will become a proud Republican, typical of the changes values and loyalties undergo in the years leading up to Montana's transformation into a state.

Virginia City, Montana. From Cemetery Hill looking south up Jackson Street, 1865-1866. Montana Historical Society Research Center Photograph Archives, Helena, Montana

MARCH

In which James Stuart leads an expedition to the Big Horn, Johnny Grant's seven children are baptized, and Charlie Russell is born.

March is the Geese Arrive Moon. It is also known as the time Napi Comes Running Down Off of the Mountains, the Moon of the Warm Chinook Winds. It is the moon of the gophers, too.

GRANVILLE STUART URGES HIS BROTHER TO COMMENCE the expedition, for time and people are pressing. Miners stampede Virginia City, and Granville knows the brothers have missed many an opportunity to score the strike that would settle them for life. Those restless gold-seekers will fan out over the Missouri, questing for the next big find. Priority is all in this enterprise—first strikers claim the best, most lucrative terrain, then write the mining laws that protect their priority.

The Stuart brothers have lived in this region on and off for seven years, ancient by standards of emigrants to this country. They had never heard of the place until they faced a desperate choice late summer of '57. On a journey from California to Iowa to visit their family, the Stuarts were caught in the maelstrom of the Mormon War, an existential battle being fought out by the Latter-Day Saints and the United States Army on the very road the brothers followed toward home. At this desperate pass, they took the word of one Jake Meek, horse and robe trader, who claimed the Beaverhead Valley was mild in winter, full of horses and game, and inhabited by friendly Indians. The Stuarts could hardly credit these claims, since they defied their experience and the logic of survival in the west, but they had little choice, and so diverted up that 300-mile path to an unknown region. They arrived via what is now called the Corinne Road, coming over the pass later named Monida into this promised land. They held their breath in wonder:

> We crossed the Rocky Mountain divide on the tenth day of October, 1857....As soon as we had crossed the divide a wonderful change appeared in the country. Instead of the gray sagebrush covered plains of Snake river, we saw smooth rounded hills and sloping bench land covered with yellow bunch grass that waved in the wind like a field of grain. A beautiful little clear stream ran northwest on its way to join the Missouri river....The forepart of October gave days of brilliant sunshine, warm and pleasant with no snow anywhere except on the tops of higher mountains and very little even there.

They didn't know it yet, but they had found home.

That winter they benefited from the abundant game and relatively mild weather promised by Meek. The Bannock Indians (the ones whose name was misspelled in naming the town of Bannack), Shoshones, Nez Perce, and Flatheads lived side-by-side, mainly engaging in horse stealing from each other and the Stuart party, an Indian practice Granville would come to know was honorable and common. The brothers spent intimate time with these Indians when the snows moved in and they were compelled to find shelter and warmth. Granville was taken by their playful sense of humor, so different from the dark, gloomy cast of mind he had assumed from all that reading in Cooper. In fact, Indian camps were scenes of practical jokes and jollity. Granville himself had been the butt of more than a few jokes, but he realized the Indians were teaching him through this

Granville Stuart, ca. 1864. Montana Historical Society Research Center Photograph Archives, Helena, Montana

mockery, always inculcating the practical lesson. He was also impressed by their sheer joy in gambling, an important winter activity to while away the hours until the snows cleared and the people could move to the buffalo grounds on the Yellowstone or Missouri river. They were especially fond of "Hands," the sleight-of-hand game in which one man rapidly shifted a bone between his hands in the hope he could fool his opponent. Granville was struck time and again by the big map the natives carried in their minds, effortlessly, laying out the entire territory of the Missouri headwaters, able to trace how the three rivers came together to form the Missouri, and the trail that took them over a divide into the Yellowstone basin, and the tributaries of that mighty river, too, the Big Horn, Rosebud, Tongue, and Powder, even though these tribes did not journey that far east very often because of the Crows, Sioux, and Cheyenne.

All of which served as prelude to the Stuarts' greatest discovery, the Deer Lodge Valley. For all the restlessness and seeking after the main chance that have defined their past seven years, they find sureness, balance, and grace in this place. There's no great mystery to the appeal: a wide, fertile valley of uncommon beauty that holds promise of gold or, short of that, of a good living in farming and ranching and trading with the many Indians that follow the "Hell Gate River" (today's Clark Fork River) to the buffalo ranges. Here they do have priority, for they join with the likes of Johnny Grant to build comfortable cabins, acquire books for winter reading, and almost casually seek the gold. Though they do not see it clearly in these terms, they are the vanguard of a transition from the fur trapping and trading economy to a new, more diversified way of making a go in this remote land. The Stuart brothers will absorb much of the experience and knowledge of the fur men and put that to work in building their own Montana lives.

As part of that education in survival, they come to appreciate a way of life that will define much of their adulthood, white men married to Indian women of various tribes. James, the older, bolder brother, will take many mates, while Granville ultimately settles on one faithful spouse, Awbonnie, a Shoshone woman who speaks fluent English. Young Mollie Sheehan, the couple's neighbor in Virginia City, is puzzled by what she calls the incongruity of the marriage between a scholarly looking white man and an Indian wife "in moccasined feet…padding about doing her simplified housekeeping." And so she asks, "Mr. Stuart, why did you marry an Indian woman?" Mr. Stuart replies, "You see, Mollie, I'm such an odd fellow. If I married a white woman she might be quarreling with me."

To Granville's credit, he learns the Shoshone tongue, as well as French, and so is able to communicate readily with the diverse characters that drift in and out of the Deer Lodge Valley. What he and James and Johnny Grant and other white men in the region come to realize is that those Indian wives not only provide pleasure and comfort, but they ease dealings with the Indians who truly control this beautiful country. While anticipating the American claim on owning the land, the Stuart brothers have no illusions about who dominates the terrain now. Sheer numbers dictate native primacy, and a steel-eyed realism about what it takes to survive assures the Indians can and will protect the place. Granville sees the folly of their ways, especially their fondness for whiskey (he and James are abstemious, unaffected by the power of liquor), their willingness to sacrifice their life source—the buffalo—for that and other trade goods, and their constant intertribal battles that will make it impossible for them to create a massed, coordinated army to resist the invaders. But for all that, he likes and admires many Indians, and he is content to inhabit their world for the time being.

But the gold madness has changed all calculations, all assumptions. The Stuarts have attempted to cash in on the boom by extracting wealth from Gold Creek in their beloved Deer Lodge Valley, but the takings have been modest. They have diversified

Awbonnie Tookanka Stuart, ca. 1864. Montana Historical Society
Research Center Photograph Archives, Helena, Montana

their earnings by operating a blacksmith shop (Granville taking the lead as smithy), running stores in Gold Creek and Bannack and, with the stampede to Virginia City, opening an establishment called Dance & Stuart, named for the joint proprietors, that supplies the miners with boots, shoes, saddles, and all manner of equipment and food. The younger, more literary and sedentary brother, Granville, is glad to man these operations while James casts about for a bigger score in gold-mad eastern Idaho. And so it is that Granville urges his brother to organize his second expedition to the Yellowstone country as early as possible in spring to get the jump on rivals.

Yet James remains strangely slow off the mark, drifty in his mind, uncertain of his course. Perhaps it is his new bride, married just this January, Ellen Lavatta, fourteen years old, of mixed Mexican and Shoshone blood. There's a passion, an intensity, an interest there that James has not displayed before in his dealings with his Indian consorts. Though Granville does not wish to press the point, Ellen must offer some special favors, since James has turned his back on his former paramour, Isabel, and her infant son.

More than romantic distractions, perhaps James holds lingering doubts based on last year's expedition to the mouth of the Big Horn on the Yellowstone River. He'd gathered his men in early April 1863, intending to search for strikes and stake a town site at the junction of those rivers. The brothers calculated that the Crows, relatively friendly, would not put up the fierce resistance anticipated from the likes of the Blackfeet and Sioux. With the valleys of the Missouri and its tributaries fast filling with emigrants, the Yellowstone looked like the next best bet for Americans of a daring cast.

In truth, the expedition never quite equaled the splendor of its conception, set forth in a formal compact:

> Having determined to explore a portion of the country
> drained by the "Yellowstone," for the purpose of discover-
> ing gold mines and securing town sites, and believing this
> object could be better accomplished by forming ourselves
> into a regularly organized company, we hereby appoint
> James Stuart captain, agreeing upon our word of honor to
> obey all orders given or issued by him or any subordinate
> officer appointed by him. In case of any member refusing
> to obey an order or orders from said captain, he shall be
> forcibly expelled from our camp. It is further understood
> and agreed, that we all do our equal portion of work, the
> captain being umpire in all cases, sharing equally the
> benefits of said labor both as to the discovery of gold and
> securing town sites.

It was a true voyage of discovery for James, however, since he
had never journeyed so far east in this country of rivers. Relying
on the maps of Lewis and Clark at the start, the expedition's captain quickly determined that following the lay of the land was
far more efficient. At one point his party spent an uncomfortable
night with a large band of Bannocks, uncomfortable because of
their penchant for stealing horses, uncomfortable when the Argonauts witnessed a scalp dance at the expense of Flathead Indians who had had the bad luck to encounter these visitors.

In the midst of their adventures, the party restlessly sur-
veyed the land for signs of gold, assessing slopes, rock types, and
"color," or traces of loose gold. Early in their travels they got a
good result in a stream soon to be called Alder Gulch, but they
were determined to move east to find a bonanza on the Yellowstone. Granville would later assert the expedition made possible
the greatest gold discovery in the region, for six explorers who
had intended to join James's party had missed a rendezvous,
been humiliated by Crows, and uncovered the jackpot quite
by chance on their return trip to Bannack. Granville protested

James Stuart. Montana Historical Society Research Center Photograph Archives, Helena, Montana

too much—he and James could not quite believe they had once again missed out on the life-altering strike. Their solace would be to write their way into the glory of the find after the fact.

On the 27th of April, the 1863 expedition confronted thirty Crow warriors who were in a mood to harass and challenge. While James conversed with three leaders through an interpreter, deploying the Shoshone language as the medium of exchange, young Crow warriors tested the party by trying to grab horses and rifles. Their ire rising, the explorers resisted, leading to wild gun fire, though little harm. That night the Crows further harried the party by stealing goods from their tents. In the morning, intent on acquiring the party's best horses, the warriors insisted on "trading" inferior stock for the expedition's superior mounts, finally causing James to tell his men to present a forceful challenge with weapons ready. Only then did the Crows relent, choosing to "ride along" with Stuart's party as it continued the journey eastward. The men were hardly comfortable in this uneasy truce. The confrontation served as foreshadowing of far worse to come.

All the while, James recorded the liabilities and assets of this (for him) new land. While the water often disappointed in its alkali flavor, the abundance of game could not but impress a seasoned hunter. When members of the expeditionary force seized the opportunity to hunt bison near Pompey's Pillar on the Yellowstone, James observed, "Buffalo to be seen in every direction, and very tame. We can ride within three hundred yards of them, unless they smell us; and if they do, they will run if they are a mile away. Small game is also abundant. No wonder the Crows like their country; it is a perfect paradise for a hunter."

At last, on the 5th of May, the expedition arrived at the junction of the Big Horn and Yellowstone rivers. James calculated a distance of 326 miles from Bannack City to the site for a projected town, Big Horn City, and he further noted it would be relatively easy to build a wagon road by the path they followed.

James Stuart was not alone in this thinking—this is precisely the route John Bozeman would trace—in fact, Bozeman and his partner passed by the expedition along the Big Horn River on their own surveying trip, but fearful after an earlier encounter with Indians, they fled from Stuart's party. Stuart's exploring party was encouraged by initial pannings for gold—they speculated they would hit a major strike farther up the Big Horn. The men then set about platting a town of 320 acres and 13 ranches of 160 acres each. They were imposing an American idea of property—the American grid—on this Crow land, marking and subdividing to assure their claim in anticipation of future development, in line with the Homestead Act just passed in 1862. They saw themselves as true civilization builders, acquiring gain while advancing their nation. In this way they were living out the vision articulated with such zeal by one of the early promoters of settlement in this seemingly undiscovered country, one J.L. Campbell, a Chicago reporter who traveled to the mines of Idaho in 1863 to see the boom for himself, then composed a guidebook for emigrants. He wrote with unfettered fervor,

> The vast adventurous army of restless and tireless gold-seekers first diffused themselves through the rich tracts of California and the Pacific coast, and has been working its way back thence toward the heart of the wilderness, until what was once laid down in the maps as an unknown waste save where sparsely investigated by various explorers, is becoming dotted with infant settlements by the magic wand of the enchanter Gold; while the region, for years abandoned as a wild for the Indian and the buffalo, is seeing the first frame work of civilized society laid across its whole extent, whereon will be built thriving and prosperous States ere the generation that first knew "the California fever" shall have passed away.

Leaving behind the imagined city, James Stuart's expedition continued south on the Big Horn. Faith in the mission peaked after encouraging signs at the mouth of the Little Big Horn: "I think we will strike it rich, for we can get plenty of colors to the pan along the river, and we are still away down in the plains." But the hopefulness of this surveying work—for gold, town, and ranches—was not to last. The inhabitants of the region would have a say in just how far these Argonauts could advance their interests and so override at least three hundred years of occupation by the Crows. Perhaps the warriors had in mind realities recorded by white observers in the region: "[T]he government agent in the area reported that 'whites are now overrunning their whole country.' These newcomers, another official reported, 'are not to be considered the purest spirits the world affords by any means.'"

On the evening of May 13, Indians—by Stuart's reckoning, Crows—fired a volley of bullets into the camp, killing two men, severely wounding two, and injuring three more slightly. Stuart barely avoided serious injury by ducking just before the hail of bullets. Samuel Hauser, a member of the expedition and later an important backer of Granville's ranching enterprise in central Montana, was seriously wounded. Horror followed upon horror, for in the morning the extent and impact of the wounds became visible. One survivor killed himself rather than endure the agony.

The surviving members of the party concluded it was no longer safe to travel in Crow country, and so they struck out for the Emigrant Road far to the south along the Sweetwater River. It became a desperate quest for home, traveling through snowy mountains, being trailed by Indians (or so they believed), and enduring the death of another comrade, who accidently shot himself. Stuart described this fatality as the most heartrending of all. At last, after another month on the trail, they arrived where they began:

After dinner, packed up and pushed on to Bannack City, which we reached late in the evening. Everybody was glad to see us, and we were glad to see everybody, although our hair and beards had grown so, and we were so dilapidated generally, that scarcely anyone knew us at first; and no wonder, for we had ridden sixteen hundred miles, and for the last twelve hundred without a tent or even a change of clothes.

Yes, Granville can understand why James might be slow off the mark in March of '64, given that epic struggle, the loss of life, and genuine fear of Indian attack. Yet the new expedition promises to shield the participants from the more terrible aspects of last year's journey, since James has gathered a much larger force, numbering near seventy-five.

At last the "army" departs for the Big Horn on March 25, but it quickly becomes evident that prospects for gold discovery will not be good. Unlike last year, the primary antagonist will be not native peoples but weather. Winter lingers, and blocks traveling and prospecting. Perhaps the sheer scale of the force gravitates against unity of purpose. In any case, James returns to Virginia City with twenty-five men on May 18, a shock to Granville and an index of the sheer futility of these grand expeditions. It will later come to light that the fifty or so men left behind by James experienced little success in their search for color and much trauma in their return. One member of the party will be found dead the next year, presumably a victim of a murderous encounter with the Crows. James's reputation as a leader of men suffers as a result. More to the point for Granville, the Stuart brothers have expended $2,000 on these efforts to "open the Yellowstone," and all they have to show for it is a platted map of a Big Horn City that remains purely fantastical, a few good stories, several lost acquaintances and friends, and bitter experience.

And so another quest for wealth will end in failure for the Stuart brothers. Granville will later lament, "It is awful to think how many d—d fools & asses are wallowing in wealth without any effort on their part to make it while we who could appreciate & use it cant possibly make a cent." James will be dead within nine years of his second Yellowstone expedition, and Granville will live a long life dedicated to celebrating his brother's achievements and eulogizing the world they had found the fall of 1857. While he could indulge in extended tributes to the pioneers who built Montana Territory, Granville will never sound fully convincing in these paeans to progress. He will be haunted by the grandeur of the place—and the freedom of the Indians—he found there on first crossing into his promised land.

On March 19, seven of Johnny Grant's children are baptized into the Catholic faith in the Deer Lodge Valley. Grant has learned the art of living life to the fullest, with many native wives, a large cattle herd that feeds the hungry miners, and frequent visits from the many nations, including and especially the Metis, truly his people, who cover a vast region with their Red River carts. The *Montana Post* describes him as "the great medicine man of the mixed French-Indian race who ranch round Deer Lodge." As son of a famous Hudson Bay trader, Richard Grant, Johnny knows the country nearly as well as the legendary Jim Bridger. He takes frequent trips south to the Oregon Trail to trade with emigrants and bring back cattle for fattening in this lush valley. He also exhibits courage on occasion, as when he journeys to the Blackfeet camps on the Marias River to negotiate, going into the country of avowed antagonists, fond of stealing his horses, to recover livestock and secure safe passage for himself and his goods. He combines luck with a *joie de vivre* not often in evidence among the sober-sided and self-interested men who risk so much to come to this country.

John T. Grant, "Johnny Grant." MONTANA HISTORICAL SOCIETY RESEARCH
CENTER PHOTOGRAPH ARCHIVES, HELENA, MONTANA

Edwin Purple, an earnest, thoughtful, careful journal-keeper
during his travels in Montana, left behind this fond tribute to
Grant, his temporary host the summer of 1862:

> John Grant, or as he is called here Johnny Grant, is a
> man I should judge of 32 or 3 years of age, tall and well
> formed, with less of the Indian than American in his fea-
> tures, of a dark swarthy complexion, increased no doubt
> by exposure and his habits of life. He had I understood
> three Indian wives, and seven or Eight, perhaps more,
> children, that he treats with an affectionate fondness
> of manner that the children of many white men might
> envy. His little son David seemed to be the more especial
> pet of his father.…Here in this luxuriant grassy valley,
> abounding with game and fish—the finest brook trout I
> ever saw—possessed of large herds of cattle and Horses,
> surrounded by his half breeds, Indian servants, and their
> families, with a half dozen old French mountaineers and
> Trappers who have married Indian women for his neigh-
> bors, Grant lives in as happy and free a manner as did the
> ancient Patriarchs.

Granville Stuart, Johnny's neighbor, will note with appreciation his weekly dances during the cabin-bound winter months.
In one of the most descriptive passages in his journals, sugges-
tive of just how much he enjoyed himself and the depth of his
nostalgia, Stuart shares this vision of a community celebration
on a snowbound January 3, 1862:

> The music for these dances was two violins; and the dance
> most popular, was the old-fashioned quadrille. The floors
> were all of puncheon hence not smooth or waxed. Some
> men called the figures. The women were Indian or half-
> breed and there were never enough to go around. A man
> with a handkerchief tied around his arm supplied the

place of a woman in some of the sets. There was much rivalry among the women of those days, as to their finery, as there is now among their white sisters. At these balls they wore their brightest calicoes with new scarlet leggings and handsomely beaded moccasins with gay plaid blankets and ornaments of feathers, shells, silver money, beads, and a generous supply of vermillion paint....It was no uncommon thing for an Indian woman to spend all of her spare time for six months, preparing a suit beaded and embroidered with colored porcupine quills, for her young son to wear to these festivities. Nor were the men without vanity. We always wore our best flannel shirt, a highly ornamented buckskin suit, and best moccasins and trimmed our hair and beards. I kept my handsomely beaded buckskin suit with its decoration of fringe until 1880 when it was stolen from my cabin on the cattle range.

No wonder Johnny Grant contracts for finishing his magnificent house in 1864, resulting in a sprawling abode by early territorial standards: "twenty three large windows, two four light windows, three transom windows. Twenty five shutters and sashes for the said windows and frames. Six batten doors...." A man of large appetites, a growing family, and many visitors must build a domicile that can serve as community hall as well as home. Though he cannot know it in this year of the territory's creation, Johnny's time in Montana will soon come to an end, largely because of the influx of so many whites who will call into question his mixed-race marriages and his distinctly un-American relish of the physical delights of life beyond the boundaries of respectability. He will transplant his sprawling, extended, multinational family to the Canadian prairies, a more tolerant place for such a card.

An artist who will shape Montana's understanding of itself is born March 19 in St. Louis. Charles Marion Russell, though raised in a respectable, well-to-do family, will find his place on the range land of his adopted territory in the 1880s. He is one of the few who can say with accuracy he knew cowboys and Indians in their authentic incarnations on the high plains of the West. He will work as nighthawk for open-range herds, a position low on the hierarchy of cowboying but one that provides an intimacy with the ways of the range that will serve him well in his art. Russell's great break as artist will come with a seemingly off-hand sketch portraying the catastrophic winter of 86-'87 that sealed the fate of open-range herds in Montana. The artist would give that famous, enduring sketch the glib but haunting title, *Waiting for the Chinook.* He later spends a few months with the Blood tribe of Blackfeet in Alberta, coming as close as possible during the reservation period to experiencing the indigenous ways of nations adapted to the Great Plains. As he tells his friend Teddy Blue Abbott, famed cowhand and rancher, "They've been living in heaven for a thousand years, and we took it away from 'em for forty dollars a month."

This elegiac note will dominate many of Russell's mature canvases, which cast a romantic light on the lives of men and women of all races who live in full contact with the physical realities of what came to be known as Russell Country, the land just east of the Rocky Mountain Front in the Great Falls area. That sentimentality will be seasoned by an assured sense of irony that will put him in the company of other great western humorists such as Will Rogers. It seems fitting that Charlie Russell's birthday coincides with that of Montana Territory.

Charles M. Russell when he was a boy. MONTANA HISTORICAL SOCIETY RESEARCH CENTER PHOTOGRAPH ARCHIVES, HELENA, MONTANA

APRIL

In which John Owen lobbies for a new territory and spring comes for the Kootenai people.

April is the Moon of the Frogs. April is the moon when the frogs come and begin their noisemaking, croaking. It is also the Moon of the Returning Bluebirds. April is also the moon when the thunder returns and all the holy bundles that pertain to the thunder are taken out to honor the return of the thunder.

RECD. A VERY KIND LETTER FROM HIS EXCELLENCY Sidney Edgerton, Govn. of Montana Ter[ritory]—Making a very handsome acknowledgement—"As he calls them" for services rend[ered] him in W. C. Spring 1864—It is true I introduced him to the Pacific Delegation—& Not only Signed but handed to Pres. Lincoln in person his application for the position he Now holds. I did Nothing More—

So writes a rotund man sitting in his library at Fort Owen in the Bitterroot Valley recalling his time in Washington City the spring of 1864. He is modest to a fault—he has provided key contacts for the men advocating creation of a new territory in the eastern portion of Idaho.

John Owen can claim priority in settling the country that became Montana, for he arrived in his beloved Bitterroot Valley in 1850. A sutler for the Army, he knew a good thing when he saw it: an incredibly beautiful valley, ideal for agriculture, and home to the friendliest of Indians, the Flathead Salish. Of average height but heavily built, Owen possessed an uncommon energy and drive. His biographer and editor claimed he covered over 23,000 miles in his years of traveling throughout the Northwest and the United States, bringing supplies to his remote home for trade with Indians and whites alike.

Owen must have been a gregarious man, judging by his voluble letters and many friends and acquaintances. It was good to be friendly and expansive in a country occupied by few whites since he established the contacts—what we would call the networks—to assure availability and delivery of the goods he needed to survive on his isolated farm. Of course, he had the good sense to purchase the Jesuits' mission in what became known as Stevensville (after the governor of Washington Territory who crafted the Hellgate or Council Grove Treaty of such importance of the Salish, Kootenai, and Pend d'Oreilles) and promptly named it Fort Owen. Like many of the other early arrivals, he relished the opportunity to imprint his name on the landscape by creating an eponymous fort or town. The Jesuit priest Father Palladino said of Owen's life in his adopted home, "Major Owen lived at the Fort like a King. He was the ruler. He always had many guests at the Fort, and was famed for his hospitality to his guests and to transient travelers who were passing through the region. He was a man of very loveable, kindly, and generous character, and the most influential pioneer in the country for years."

Nancy, a Shoshone woman, had been Owen's companion since before his arrival in the Bitterroot, and they apparently had a long, tranquil relationship. They formally wed in a modest ceremony in 1858, a rare display of respect for a native wife in that country at that time. No doubt in part because of this relationship, Owen often expressed deep sympathy and respect for his native neighbors. That rapport would be a major reason

Major John Owen; builder and founder of Fort Owen. MONTANA HIS-
TORICAL SOCIETY RESEARCH CENTER PHOTOGRAPH ARCHIVES, HELENA,
MONTANA

he was named Special Agent to the Flathead Salish in 1856. He frequently acknowledged the aboriginals' rights under common decency and treaties, and he complained bitterly at times of the United States government's mistreatment of his neighbors. Yet similar to the principles behind the Sun River Indian Farm, Owen espoused the importance of inculcating an agricultural life in native minds. Toward that goal he urged providing livestock and farming implements to ease their way toward a yeoman life.

That this strong-willed if likeable Owen should be a main agent of Montana Territory's creation was ironic from any number of perspectives, not the least of which being his oft-stated vitriol for a government that could not uphold its annuity or territorial obligations to the native people. As he wrote Superintendent of Indian Affairs Edward Geary on May 25, 1860, "I fear the Indians will not be satisfied in having so large an amount of property a great deal of which is perfectly useless forced upon in payment for their lands, without their consent ever being asked or obtained." Compounding that irony were Owen's incendiary views of the Republican administration, and above all, Abraham Lincoln. In a letter addressed to an Illinois Congressman who stood on the floor of the House to defend General George McClellan against calumny and to attack the drift toward redefining the War of the Rebellion as a means to end slavery, this Union Democrat railed,

> What a dark political resurrection awaits [Lincoln] & his Constitutional advisers. The history of this unhappy Crusade is yet to be Written in letters of Blood. The people of this remote & Mt. Locked Section [of the] Country are devoted to the Union. There is No Sacrifice they would Not Make for its peaceful restoration. But Mr L[incoln']s policy is Not the one We advocate. The brave McClelland Must be Superseded for the Simple reason that the Eman-

cipation act was two bitter a pill for his Constitutional pallate.

It is helpful to recall that McClellan was a notably ineffective field commander, and that as a Democrat himself, he espoused beliefs such as this: "Help me to dodge the nigger—we want nothing to do with him. I am fighting to preserve the integrity of the Union....To gain that end we cannot afford to mix up the negro question."

Whatever his views of the president, Owen took that long, arduous journey to the nation's capital to advance the cause of a new territory. He would be away fifteen months, stopping to visit his family in Pennsylvania and delayed by a companion's illness and bad weather. In his absence his fort will be managed by one Thomas W. Harris, whose journal for 1864 suggests a man more than little over his head with the duties of stewardship over Owen's property and business interests. Harris's fecklessness provides an index of the absentee owner's strengths. His neglectful caretaking will lead to a lawsuit upon the owner's return. In fairness, Harris attends to the grist mill Owen had built at great expense to grind the flour that would convert wheat to profit, transports wheat to nearby Hell Gate, and cares for the seventy head of cattle belonging to the absent master. He also attempts to fill the void of hospitality left by the affable Owen, hosting a dinner on Christmas Day, 1863, and a dance on the 1st of January, 1864.

In his run of work and hosting, Harris witnesses the backwash of extralegal remedies, since he reports yet another instance of vigilante justice at the fort on the 26th of January: "This morning the Vigilance party left with their prisoner went about two miles below the fort and left him Swinging to a Pine Limb this they Say is the twentieth man they have hung within the last two month and if Zackry is caught he is twenty one." And through his eyes we see the increasing pace of life in the new territory when he notes of the nearby trading center, "The pack trains & emigrants are passing Hellgate all the time 5 trains passed up from Lewistown yesterday."

Toward the end of '64 and the beginning of '65, Harris's longing for Owen's return surfaces with increasing urgency. Weary of the responsibility for the Major's business, and worried about the fate of the peripatetic man, he records rumors that Owen has been killed by Sioux on his return journey. While expressing doubts about those rumors, his anxiety is manifest in his forced heartiness and too-frequent speculations about the Major's whereabouts. Perhaps compounding Harris's concern are occasional visits from Owen's wife, Nancy, suggesting her loneliness and apprehension.

In the end, of course, John Owen does return. At last, on February 12, 1865, Harris nearly chortles,

> This evening Mr. Collins came out from Fort to bring the glad news of Maj Owens arrival. God knows I am truely glad he is Safe at home as it takes a great responsibility off of my Shoulders, which I have had for the last 16 months being in charge of the Fort.

As it happens, Owen had been on a challenging adventure during the fall of '64—he had joined Jim Bridger's second expedition skirting the western flank of the Big Horn Mountains.

In his hand-written "Diary of a Journey from the North Platte to Montana in 1864," Owen shows the grind, tedium, and frustration of driving cattle and wagons over untested ground following Bridger's preferred route to the mines. The legendary mountain man and guide had conceived this alternative to what became known as the Bozeman Trail because he recognized the threat to prime hunting grounds for the Sioux and Cheyenne along the Powder River. Bridger was acting on bitter experience with the nations that claimed the region as their own. By the time Owen followed him into Montana, Bridger had become

Jim Bridger. MONTANA HISTORICAL SOCIETY RESEARCH CENTER PHOTO-
GRAPH ARCHIVES, HELENA, MONTANA

a living legend, surrounded by tall tales of his adventures, especially surviving Indian attack.

In reality, "Old Gabe" was an experienced, careful, respected guide who had spent more than forty years in the northern and central Rockies, trapping, trading, guiding, and coming to know the vast region better than any American. He combined a calm, reassuring manner with uncommon qualities that increased his chances of survival. Wilderness-smart though poorly educated, brave but not foolhardy, adventurous but willing to find a strategic retreat when conditions required, he had outlived many of his contemporaries in the fur business. His unusual moniker, "Old Gabe," given to him by another legendary mountain man who died an early death, Jedediah Smith, compares the seasoned mountain man to the angel Gabriel, the revealer of God's truth to human beings. The title is meant to suggest Bridger's unusual clarity of mind and insight, delivered to those who trusted him with sureness but not arrogance.

Like so many of the other key white men living in the region in 1864, including Owen himself, Bridger had taken native women as wives: a Flathead daughter of a chief, a Utah woman, and a Shoshone daughter of a chief. These relationships sealed his connection to the friendlier tribes in his adopted home, and also provided him with comfort and a family. However, in a sobering revelation of the realities of life in this place and time, two of his wives had died in childbirth. Bridger's relationships with the Flathead, Shoshone, Crow, and Utah in part explain his remarkable durability. He developed a profound intimacy with tribal nations, coming to know their needs and desires, sensitive to pressure points that could yield conflict, sensing those moments or gestures that would result in battle.

Certainly Old Gabe had lived his share of adventures. He is credited with being the first white man to "discover" the Great Salt Lake; he shot the Big Horn Canyon and so earned the lasting respect of the Crows; he was one of the first Americans to uncover the wonder of what is now Yellowstone Park; and he encountered many a hostile war party, especially Blackfeet, Sioux, Cheyenne, and Arapaho, and lived to tell about those encounters. In one of those classic passages handed down to us through the scattered, fragmentary glimpses provided by contemporary journals and letters, he is said to have made light of carrying two arrowheads in his body for over a year: "In the mountains the meat never spoils!"

Bridger is also credited with finding the path over South Pass that made the Oregon Trail possible, even inevitable. And so, once again, charismatic figures out of 1864 raise perplexing questions about purpose and desire. Given his own intimacy with native peoples, what did he make of his helping unleash this flood of emigration that changed the world of the northern Rockies forever? It's tempting to conclude that Bridger, like his compatriots, followed the profit motive, for he established a trading post on the Trail that provided him a comfortable living, underwriting a fine Missouri farm to which he would retreat annually for recreation. It's also possible the guide was placing a bet, anticipating that this surge of Americans would favor some tribes, his closest friends, and disempower the hostile nations that had challenged him and his indigenous allies. In any case, he would live to see the consequences of this invasion, even in the seemingly most protected and impenetrable of places, the headwaters of the Missouri.

Bridger's Cut-off has come down to us in legendary style, rife with stories of a race with Bozeman to determine the best way to get to the Montana diggings in a hurry. In truth, it was no contest: As Owen's journal makes clear, this path was too hard on animals, wagons, and human beings to offer a practical alternative, a reality that would lead to what became known as Red Cloud's War along the Bozeman Trail. To take an example from Owen's scribbled impressions, in an entry dated September 21, early in the journey, he writes:

Traveled 8 Miles & camped on a dry stream country hilly
and barren in the extreme no sign of vegetation except
Sage & grease wood found enough of the former[.]…sa-
line water for stock and but a poor supply of grass…"

Owen was called upon to care for a sick traveler, a Mr. Parham, whose illness would persist throughout the arduous trek
to Montana, and thus delay Owen's return to the Bitterroot. The
company was clearly fortunate to be led by Bridger, for as one
entry records,

> "Bridger Bagd a fine Bul Antelope We have plenty of fresh
> Buffaloe Sign & am in hourly Expectation of having a fat
> cow Killd & brought into Camp Bridger Killd two Bulls
> Some days since.…

In a sobering reminder of the implicit threat of traveling
through country long dominated by competing tribal nations,
Owen adds,

> Mr Parham & Myself remaind back to bring up the rear
> of the train & guard it against any Stragling Indians that
> Might feel like Committing depredations.

Owen's last entry in this truncated journal captures the ennui
and strain of the overland wagon train (his editor observes that
this entry was written in a hand indicative of heavy drinking):

> Tuesday Nov 1st The cattle Lost not being found rqrd
> some change in both loads to move on So the Camp to-
> day has spent it with the Wagons &c &c—Mr. Parham on
> his piss again all right.

Owen's joy upon recovering his lost world erupts in his first
entry for 1865:

> in fact from the Manner in Which they greeted Me af-
> ter hearing of My return Made Me truly feel as though I

belonged to the Country—I found my old friend Major
Wm. Graham here looking well as usual—Mr. Harris &
family I found well also My old Wife who Seemed de-
lighted to see Me after hearing the Many reports of My
Capture & Massacre by the Indians on the Waters of the
[Missouri] river....

He would remain anchored in this cherished home for
another six years, witnessing but not participating in the gold
rush that resulted in many more settlers—and many more
native-white conflicts—than he had known in his first fourteen
years in the once-remote valley. By 1871 he had drifted into the
early stages of dementia, no doubt caused, at least in part, by
his heavy drinking. Though he would live to 1889, he would
never recover the faculties that had allowed him to become one
of the first Americans to find sanctuary in the place now called
Montana.

THE KOOTENAI CULTURE COMMITTEE TEACHES:

Spring was the season when bears came out of their caves,
hungry for many of the same roots that fed the people.
Children were taught to be careful about how they talked
about bears and what they called them. Many teachings
come from bears.

Migratory birds, especially ducks, swans, cranes and
geese, provided good variety to the spring diet. A group
activity was to scare ducks off the water and then to catch
them in a net. Picture a lightweight, portable soccer goal.
Leo Williams remembers that two people would hold the
light poles with a net stretched in between, while another
would drive the ducks in that direction. When the ducks
started flying, after running along the water, then low

above the ground, the people would catch them in the net.

Eggs were treasured. Female geese start laying eggs during the first weeks of March and continue as late as June, along with ducks, around the same time. Canada geese typically nest on the ground on islands and shorelines, laying about six eggs, one per day. Males are very aggressive in protecting the nest, making egg collecting a potentially dangerous activity. Duck nests, although more difficult to find, are easier to rob....

Early spring was a time when people could catch whitefish with their bare hands. Vernon Finley explains that when you stood in the water of a lake where a river was feeding in near the reeds, the water was dirty from the snowmelt coming in, but people could feel the whitefish bumping up against their legs and could grab them and throw them out of the water. The northwest side of Flathead Lake (Somers) was a favorite place to take fish this way. Depending on the take and the need, some of the fish, along with their roe, were dried separately and stored for future use. The inlet of Lake McDonald provided a similar opportunity for late winter fishing.

Arrow-Leaf Balsamroot (Balsamorhiza sagittata) stems provided a fresh treat somewhat like celery. Fresh greens were especially appreciated after the long winter. The tender new shoots of balsamroot also provide important food for deer and elk in the spring.

With the receding snow, antlers shed the previous fall were gathered for many useful purposes. Some of the important tools included the antler-handled digging sticks women used for roots, and antler knapping tools of both elk and deer that men used for making knives and projectile points for hunting.

MAY

In which James Vail tells the story of his failed mission at Sun River Indian Farm, the Salish gather the bitterroot and negotiate a treaty, and President Lincoln signs Montana Territory into existence.

———————

May is the Moon of the Green Grass. It begins to grow, comes out of the ground, it also is the moon of leaves, when the leaf begins to appear on the growth. It is also the moon that changes the color on some certain animals, when the summer color comes on. It is known too for the pretty flowers blooming.

———————

OUR HOPES ARE BLASTED. Torrential rains and the waters raging out of the Rocky Mountains three times cause the Sun River Indian Farm to flood this May, all crops ruined.

We came to the upper Missouri with such faith in 1862, my wife, Martha Jane, her sister, Electa Bryan, our two young children, Mary and Harvey, and myself, James Vail. Our minister, Henry Reed, offered us this opportunity when he was appointed Indian agent to the Blackfeet and Gros Ventres. The Sun River Indian Farm was built to demonstrate the practicality and virtues of a settled agricultural life for the wild Blackfeet tribes, a provision of the Blackfeet Treaty of 1855. It would also serve as an Indian school, bringing enlightenment through secular and sacred texts to our dusky brothers. We felt the call to help the Indians learn the ways of civilization and Christianity. We heard the skepticism of many onboard our steamer, who openly declaimed they put little faith in the success of our enterprise. Unlike those doubters, we believe the Indians possess souls but must be brought to the light. As a teacher of eighteen months in Iowa, I knew my ability to move even the most recalcitrant student to improve.

We embarked for Fort Benton from St. Louis on May 14 in that second year of war on the riverboat Emilie, Captain Joseph La Barge commanding. With 150 passengers and full of supplies and equipment for the mining camps, as well as provisions for the Indian tribes, it appeared an unsinkable craft, yet at times our steamer seemed a frail bark on those fickle waters as we churned against the surging waters of the spring rise and the stiff winds out of the west. Those powerful waters reminded us that sublime mountains rose to the west, capturing snow and feeding rivers. We would soon be living in the shadow of those peaks. We were comforted by the knowledge that our riverboat was preceded by a sister craft, the Shreveport, lighter, faster, and so able to navigate the shallow waters of the upper Missouri during the dry summer months. Since this steamer left nearly a month before us, we did not anticipate seeing her until reaching Fort Union at the junction with the Yellowstone River. We were also reassured by the company of distinguished men on board our boat, most notably the partners in The American Exploring and Mining Company. One of their leaders, Francis Thompson, would prove a dear friend during our trials on the upper Missouri.

The first stage of the journey through the state of Missouri provoked thoughts of our national strife, the War of the Rebellion. We witnessed burned-out cabins, fields destroyed by fighting men and fire, cannon and rifles discarded as though flung by dying arms. Much of St. Joseph had been blackened by fire and destruction. At night, while smoking my evening cigar, listening to the steady rhythm of the river coursing against our docked steamer, I often found myself meditating on the purpose of our journey in a time of war. I could not escape the conviction we sought a new beginning, a kind of utopia, I suppose, as far removed from the meanness and intractability of those contending forces as possible. This seemed true for most on board the Emilie, though some had far more material motives than we, motives only fueled by tales told by mountain men streaming downriver toward St. Louis with animal skins and news of the glorious gold mines and the vision of emigrants striking out for the mines on the Oregon Trail as we passed Omaha.

I worried most about Electa, slight, intelligent, and naïve. When she implored us to join this great adventure, we could hardly fault her, yet fear for her we did. Electa pleaded that she could watch and tutor our children, do her share of farm chores, help teach the Indian school, and provide assistance should Martha Jane face the prospect of bringing forth another life. However, if Mrs. Vail and I saw the journey as a mission, a spiritual trial, Electa viewed it as a chance to leave behind the tedium, routines, and tensions of her family's small Ohio town. We knew that we might expose her to danger with the Blackfeet, a notoriously unpredictable tribe, as strong and fickle as the Missouri. We did not anticipate other dangers in the form of a charming stranger of her own race.

As the steamer churned west and north we met various tribes, most notably a camp of one hundred Sioux lodges, the men impressive in their breech clouts and blankets, the women less imposing but attractive in their skin shirts and leggings covered with beads. Through these encounters with the original Americans I understood fully for the first time how much the Indians depend upon our civilized goods, metal pots and spoons, cloth, sugar and coffee, and ammunition. The Americans and Indians eagerly take part in this intercourse, these transactions of robes and goods, yet I wondered whether this was the means to end the enmity, to bring about a lasting peace on the plains. Could trade pacify the tribes? When I saw how the Sioux grabbed so greedily for the annuities, I realized that contention over these very goods could only spur violence within and between the tribes. There was something demeaning about the way American supplies served as a sop and temptation to the red men. The river proved a caravan of wonders, a spectacle of contrasting humanity. If I was confronted with a painted warrior one moment, the next an aromatic, bearded mountain man drifted by in his mackinaw, his craft weighed down with robes, smoking his pipe as though he were reading the newspaper by the fireplace on an Iowa farm. And then there were the rebels, the seceshes, onboard the Emilie, who often spoke bitterly of the unjust war and their right to form a more perfect union. Their lips dripped with scorn for our president, and I must politely put them off, walk away before coming to blows. Even a man of faith has limits on his tolerance for such treason. They told me they go west to make their own little republics, built on their southern principles. I suspected they were cowards fleeing the fight, and their talk compensated for their lack of action. Among this motley humanity, Mrs. Vail and I were especially grateful for the presence of Reverend John Francis, an eloquent Welchman who led Sunday services with vigor and grace. It was such a comfort to suspend the cares of travel and the uncertainty of what the future might hold by joining his services anchored in the Bible. Even the roughest of passengers took note and observed the Sabbath in some quiet manner. For a day at least the war in the States and among the travelers was all but forgotten.

A man from Iowa could not help but be struck by the fecundity of nature the farther we journeyed from St. Louis. Antelope, deer, and elk in profusion, a grizzly bear on occasion, and the ravenous, predatory wolves moving in confident packs. What a grand sight to see the buffalo on these prairies, roaming wild in their homeland. Some of the passengers fired at the often stoic beasts, felling one now and then and sharing the meat tasting of the wild country. It was sobering to see many buffalo corpses floating downstream on the high water, nature culling the herd. We heard talk that the buffalo had decreased greatly in number over the past two decades as settlers move west and the Indians killed more and more for trade with the whites. I found such talk incredible in light of what I witnessed on our river trip.

We had the good fortune to discover our minister and guide, Mr. Reed, at Fort Berthold, where he held a grand council with Sioux complaining vociferously of traders supplying tribes upriver with guns and ammunition that are used to attack these very Indians. We were comforted by Mr. Reed's warmth, his enthusiastic thanks for our willingness to serve his calling as Indian agent to the affiliated Blackfeet tribes. Sadly, all his good intentions would not spare us the pain of our endeavors in this wild country.

What a spectacle these Indians provided. When buffalo were shot by passengers, Sioux men, women, and children streamed onboard the Emilie to gorge themselves on liver, stomach, kidneys, and brain, all raw and bloody. My children turned away in horror, but I assured them this was the custom of these people, one that would improve with time and instruction.

Upriver from Fort Berthold we witnessed the first of many examples of competition for control of trade in our new home. Our craft and the Spread Eagle, a steamer in the service of the American Fur Company, the established rival to the backers of the Emilie, engaged in a race for priority on the Missouri. When our steamer took the lead, the opposing craft rammed us, causing many onboard the Emilie to grab rifles and threaten to shoot the pilot and his crew on the Spread Eagle. The antagonistic steamer drifted back, conceding a temporary defeat. So it is that greed drives men to desperate means, so it is that even good people can be made barbarous by the quest for wealth in a new country.

After we passed Fort Union, we felt the swiftness and might of the Missouri all the more. We stopped often to wood since the increasing flood strained the Emilie's boilers. For a time we had been out of sight of our sister steamer, the Shreveport, and we felt some desire for companionship as we entered sere country of broken rocks and rattlesnakes. Big horn sheep occasionally peeked out shyly from the tan cliffs and narrow valleys. Their odd eyes could unsettle even a seasoned farmer, familiar with the ways of animals domestic and feral.

It was with great relief that we came alongside the Shreveport just past the mouth of the Judith River. Hallooing and "hail fellow, well met" ensued. It was the first time in many days that my dear wife shared her warm smile. Mary, Harvey, and Electa danced a jig. Yet how the rapids challenged our crafts, compelling many of us to walk along the broken shore in mud, rain, and chill. At times we took the ropes and cordelled our boats over rapids, directing them to the still water near shore. No wonder ours would be among the first steamers to reach Fort Benton during the almost sixty years of American presence in this distant region. The good Reverend Francis preached on "Faith and Works," a most appropriate theme for the mud-splattered, bedraggled passengers who truly earned their way to the upper reaches of this vast country.

I shall never forget the wonder of the white cliffs as we neared our destination. Nature is God's cathedral, never more so than when His hand carves stone to such sublime effects. Several of us scrambled to the top of the cliffs despite the blustery weather and were rewarded with a view of magnificent mountains to the south and west. I felt truly blessed at that moment.

Reaching Fort Benton, our hearts soared, even as the difficulty of our task sunk deep. This port of call is but an adobe fort and thrown-together wooden buildings along the river. We noted locals call the place Benton City, a grandiose term, no doubt a hopeful anticipation of the city to be, the St. Louis of the upper Missouri. Still, we adopted this usage as our own. We had the good fortune to be greeted by Little Dog, whom we took to be

the chief of all the Blackfeet. Short but powerfully built, he wore
the blue coat of an Army officer. He presented a friendly countenance, telling us through our translator that he would send out
messengers to his people's camps, encouraging them to come to
Benton to trade for the goods our intrepid steamer had delivered. Little Dog gave me hope that our model farm could alter
the Indians' views of farming.

We soon formed a party to embark for the Sun River: the Vail
family, Francis Thompson, Joseph Swift, a young fellow who
agreed to work with us, and Major Reed. Since the weather had
turned warm, even hot, we had a pleasant two-day jaunt across
the prairie, the Rocky Mountains looming closer and closer as
we approached the Sun River.

The farm did not present a promising face. It was in truth
a fort, the palisaded walls and rough cabins made out of aging, cracked cottonwood. The only caretaker for the place for
many months had been an Indian named Iron, who could not
prevent the theft of many implements and horses by our native neighbors. As Francis drily noted, there were few Indians
taking instruction in farming. Since it was already late June, I
puzzled over how to make good use of this first summer in our
new home. We decided to concentrate our energies on starting
a garden, planting a few acres of oats and wheat, and serving as
a lesson in respectable, cultivated behavior for what we hoped
would be many swarthy guests.

But I get ahead of myself, discounting the pleasures of being
in our new home in a new country with charming visitors. Major Reed exuded his typical energy and electrical spirit, walking
the banks of the Sun River, declaiming to the sky of God's glory
in the shadow of those stunning, irregular peaks to the west.
Francis told stories of his life as a banker back east, meeting re-
luctant clients and teaching them the errors of their ways, but
above all, nearly dancing with glee at the prospect of opening his
business in Bannack and breathing the mountain air that could

be a tonic for bad lungs. Young Swift would prove a godsend in his dogged determination, his willingness to stay by our sides through trying times, yet he could not protect us from a snake within. No one could.

Our next order of business was to repair the broken ferry that was so vital to taking men, wagons, animals, and material across the still-powerful Sun. Reed, Thompson, Swift, and I set about this simple but protracted task. We then witnessed Mr. Thompson's departure for the mines. He evinced joy and a bit of trepidation at casting his lot with fate. That vast country swallowed a man slowly as he rode south on the Mullan Road, and when at last we lost all vision of our friend, I felt the emotion rising in my throat, for all the time we had been together on the Emilie, our visits with Indians of all stripes, the cordelling, the songs sung and prayers shared. We could only hope to see that good man again.

We settled into our routine for that first summer: Joseph and I repaired the plow, tilled the soil, and planted the crops; Martha Jane and Electa put the buildings in order, bringing a woman's sense of order and grace to those graceless cabins; the children, just two and four years of age, learned the art of amusing themselves in a wilderness, catching dragon flies, tracking harmless snakes, and building their own small versions of our fortress farm with sticks and stones. Major Reed commenced his duties as Indian agent, traveling to Benton City on occasion and visiting with Little Dog and other friendly Indians. The Blackfeet chief had created his own small farm just a few miles from us, though his crops fared little better (in fact, worse) than ours. We were fortunate to benefit from the skill of Iron, who interpreted Little Dog's words, supplied wild game, and cared for the livestock. All he asked in return was an opportunity to share our meals and smoke the pipe. These were requests easily fulfilled. We read the Bible much together, kept our eyes sharp for unexpected visitors, and reminded ourselves daily of the purpose of this long journey into these wild, untamed lands. When Indians approached us singly or in numbers, my heart jumped to my throat, for I was not used to confronting them in this isolated place with my family so exposed. Most often they were hunting or traveling to meet with others of their kind, but they would stop out of curiosity, peer into our doorways and windows, grunt with satisfaction or doubt. Our good hunter could communicate with them through signs and later explained their intentions. Tribesmen of all kinds passed by our fort, Piegan, Flathead, Bannock, and Nez Perce. Our farm was located on a very old road leading from the mountains to the plains, the means for tribes living west of the mountains to journey to the land of buffalo. Even a man untutored in Indian ways could see a kind of wonder in our dusky guests as they left behind the narrow mountain passes for the sweeping prairie, as though the sky opened up for them and showed a new, expansive world.

Perhaps, then, it should not have surprised me that we saw little evidence of interest in our work, especially as the crops were struggling due to late planting and scalding sun, and our lives seemed sedentary and vexing to men and women used to a nomadic life. Only Little Dog continued to evince an interest in our work, though we sensed he paid a price in scorn from his people.

Soon enough the river overflowed its banks following torrential rains. Our meager crops were overwhelmed by the mountain waters. Garter snakes and muskrats plagued our cabins. Our monotonous days were broken by emigrants following the Mullan Trail to and from Benton City. More than one sojourner hinted at possessing gold garnered in Bannack, gold they carried back to the States to claim a new life. There were ruffians as well, hard-faced and hard-spoken men who looked at my wife and sister-in-law with impudent familiarity. It was not those mysterious natives alone who caused me concern. I said a prayer each time such rough company continued on the trail.

The weather turned golden in September, the aspens and cottonwoods yellow-leafed in the south-turning sun. The river receded at last, yet it was too late to save our oats and wheat. As the first frosts coated our cabins in early October, I came to fear the grip of winter. No doubt travelers on the Mullan would diminish with no prospect of finding passage back to the States. Major Reed had already taken a craft down the Missouri to obtain the Blackfeet annuities for the following spring. As I looked about, considering our isolated situation and just Swift, Iron, and myself to fend off threats, I wondered whether I might find an extra hand in Benton to carry the burden of protection through the long winter. In truth, I held out little hope of finding such a man, yet ride to Benton I did with a kind of quiet desperation.

Imagine my wonder and relief to discover not one but two men interested in my proposition: Henry Plummer and Jack Cleveland. They had passed us quickly on their way to Benton only a week earlier. They were a study in contrasts. Plummer was a true gentleman in countenance, dress, and speech, though maimed fingers on his left hand suggested a harder life than one might suppose on first acquaintance. He stood about five feet ten with brown hair and grey eyes. He was an easy conversationalist, eager with stories of his travels and adventures in California and Washington. He was a man one could easily like. Cleveland presented a more threatening appearance, rough around the edges and often vulgar in his speech. I could not conceive how these two came to be partners on the road, but when I asked if they would be willing to spend the winter at Sun River Indian Farm, they readily agreed. They had arrived in Benton with the expectation of transportation to St. Louis, only to discover that travel by mackinaw was not recommended due to the threat posed by the Sioux. Our humble farm presented a much finer prospect than the bleak port town.

Reactions varied when I arrived with our two guests. Martha Jane was dismayed at having two men—particularly Cleveland—in close proximity during winter confinement; Joseph showed delight at the prospect of male companionship; Harvey and Mary believed they had found two new objects of study; and Electa grew very quiet. A small, clever woman, Electa had that unusual ability to become large or small depending on the occasion. One moment one might not be aware she was in the room, and the next she roared like a lion. I had learned that when she grew quiet, she was not so much withdrawing her attention as focusing it. Certainly our guests took notice of her, particularly Plummer.

A brother-in-law is often the last to know or understand in these cases. My eyes averted, concentrated on Cleveland to determine whether he was acting properly, the daily chores of caring for our horses and cattle, and our children staying warm in their restless forays into the wind-driven cold of high-plains early winter days, I did not detect the deep affection growing between Electa and Plummer. Martha Jane hinted at times, hoping that I would intervene and discourage such a connection. We had all fallen half in love with Henry, for he seemed a decent man with a hard life. He did not conceal some of his brushes with violence and the law in California. It was the need for human companionship during those days enclosed in our snug cabin—he told stories to pass the time and to give us a glimpse into his life. It was not unlike Othello telling his tales of war to Desdemona.

Electa began to attend to him in a way I had never seen in her. There was no great mystery to the attraction between them. For a talented young teacher from a scattered family in Ohio, living in the wilds of Dakota Territory with an Indian for hunter and Indians for occasional guests, perhaps such a fixation or attraction was natural. Yet I presumed the difference in their experience would dissuade a more enduring relationship. Not being romantic myself, I did not anticipate the course of their affection. Cleveland grew more peevish and irritable as the bond between Electa and Henry came clear. One time as Henry and I were feeding the stock hay he told me of his strained relationship with his traveling companion, hinting at deeper causes. I could sense the reasons for it. Jack could be boisterous and even playful with the children, and he could be surprisingly gentle with Martha Jane. But he emanated a restless energy that demanded outlet. At times his language and manners slipped, revealing a hidden nature rough and untamed. I had no doubt he had harmed other human beings. Still the mystery of his connection to Henry remained. We would not be sorry to see Cleveland depart for points east in the spring.

Yet depart he and Henry did not. This is the moment I must admit to my own culpability, my role in this tragic play. I tolerated the growing affection between Plummer and Electa, and it was that very bond that persuaded Henry to remain in the region. Rather than taking the first mackinaw east to St. Louis, he would stay to marry my sister-in-law. How many lives would have been spared the agony of what followed had I acted the proper part of a guardian and guide and prevented that engagement. I cannot plead ignorance of that option, for Martha Jane drove it home to me with increasing fervor. She told me she was heartsick at the prospect of her sister marrying this stranger arriving as if by magic out of his troubled past.

In late November, as fear of Indian predation receded since they were in their winter camps, Plummer and Cleveland prepared to journey to Bannack City, with Henry's promise of returning in spring to complete the nuptials. I was relieved to see them go, yet troubled by the prospect of that summer wedding. Martha Jane and I vowed to do our best to break off the engagement.

We were aided by the unexpected return of Francis Thompson in May. He had taken a grand journey to the Pacific coast and had just returned to what was now Idaho Territory. But he had a frightening tale to tell of Mr. Plummer, now sheriff at Bannack, gleaned during his travels: By Francis's account, Plummer had shot Cleveland dead in a barroom brawl instigated by Henry's fear his traveling companion would disclose some compromising information about him. It seemed a cold-blooded act, compounded by Plummer's attempt to lure another citizen of Bannack into a gunfight simply because that man may have heard Cleveland's dying confession implicating the sheriff. The agitated Francis urged my sister-in-law to delay the wedding, return east for a time, and marry in the fall if that remained her desire. At first Electa fought against this argument, expounded on Plummer's virtues and the envy of lesser men, and said that she would renounce her family before her fiancé. But when Martha Jane joined forces with Francis and me, Electa's resolve weakened. She viewed her sister as her guide, the long-time source of comfort and wisdom. Yes, she said, yes, she would return east at the first opportunity, then await the verdict of her heart.

But there was to be no such opportunity. Plummer arrived on June 2, earlier than anticipated, and all of young Electa's determination to delay dissolved. Oh no, it was a fervent, moving reunion, that I must admit. I must recall that Henry, for all of his worldly experience, was only 27, and Electa but 21. We extracted a promise to delay the nuptials until Major Reed returned to the fort, but when he had not arrived by June 20, I agreed to ask a priest at the nearby St. Peter's Mission to perform the service. That was a challenge unto itself for devout Methodists, but there seemed no deferring the union.

June 20, 1863, the cusp of the longest day of the year, proved a wonder of light and warmth on the Sun River. Martha Jane refused to participate in the ceremony as her sister's brides-

maid, withdrawing instead to her room to weep. Adding an almost farcical touch to the tragic proceedings, Francis stood in
as Electa's maid, while Joseph performed the part of best man.
No one could deny the bride and groom illuminated the room
with their joy. Electa was dressed in simple brown calico, yet
her eyes shone with emotion and her smile proved irrepressible.
Henry appeared in a blue suit that displayed his manly form. Oh
no, I could not doubt their fitness for each other in ways spiritual and material. Father Joseph Manatre performed his lengthy
Catholic service, but it did not seem tedious or idolatrous there
in our humble cabin. The cross-currents of emotion pushed
me through the event as though I were on a frail bark descend-
ing the flooding Sun. We were all riding that frail bark. After a
wedding breakfast of buffalo hump and corn bread, the happy
couple rode a government ambulance pulled by four wild Indian
ponies south toward their new life in Bannack City.

It was but two months before we would join them, much to
our surprise. The summer devolved into a cascade of crises, every bit as fluid and powerful as the Great Falls of the Missouri
we had visited earlier in June. First was the increasing threat of
Indian violence, our fears only compounded when Joseph ab-
sconded to the mining metropolis as Francis's assistant. We were
doubly fearful since our loyal hunter Iron had been murdered
by Bannack Indians earlier in the spring, our interpreter and
hunter now departed for the afterlife. We had grown so fond of
this kind, reliable guide. He was a gentle soul. He deserved better. We could never quite sort out the tribal conflicts that took
his life.

Compounding our sense of loss, the brutally hot conditions
meant our crops had no chance to survive. The land was so
parched that we drove our cattle and horses to higher ground
in the shadow of the Rocky Mountains since the livestock had
the benefit of flowing streams and lush grasses there. When Major Reed failed to return by August, we concluded the Missouri

was too low to allow even the Shreveport to pass Cow Island two hundred miles east of Benton. Our minister sent word via emigrants that he would not bring supplies and livestock to support the farm. Our fear and weariness turned to despair at this news. The Piegan would surely become increasingly restless and resentful since they would not receive the annuities promised them by treaty. Our fortified farm could seem an apt target for their rage. It was not easy to concede defeat, yet defeat it was. We had arrived at Sun River Indian Farm the summer before with high hopes of transforming the farm and the wild people who lived nearby. We had failed at both tasks. We had as well lost dear Electa to a man with a past as checkered as the shirts he wore so vainly. As Martha Jane and I considered our choices, we arrived at a surprising conclusion: Why not join Electa in Bannack? We still had some capital from our sale of the farm in Iowa, thus I could purchase a home for us in the mining town. I might try my hand at prospecting, and Martha Jane could serve as sister and confidant to Electa. It was, in the end, a great relief to load our few worldly goods and follow the Mullan south, then trace the Missouri to the Madison and on to Bannack.

We were like most emigrants first coming to that wide open town sprung like magic from the rocky ground: stimulated, amused, and perplexed. Bannack was a collection of rough-hewn cabins, makeshift stores, and loud hurdy-gurdy houses. The division between Northerners and Southerners was written in the layout of the town, for Yankee Flats bespoke its denizens' political leanings. We rented a cabin in the Flats, and Martha Jane played hostess to her sister and brother-in-law, as well as cook for Francis and Joseph. It was apparent that gold remained a prospect in that valley, leading me to take up a claim and try my hand at sluicing gold.

Electa and Henry seemed companionable, even joyful at times, yet some undercurrent of awkwardness or doubt would on occasion surface. Their whispers communicated more anguish than intimacy, as though they were contemplating a dramatic action that carried risk. At last they disclosed the direction of their thoughts: Electa would return to Iowa to await Henry's joining her. Martha Jane expressed our surprise, even bafflement, yet the explanation was vague. Electa pleaded the couple's desire to establish a respectable life, including children, and Bannack City was hardly the setting for such a marriage. While this explanation was plausible, it was hardly satisfying. Why did not Sheriff Plummer simply accompany my sister-in-law on her journey? Why risk separation at all? Despite our best efforts to extract a fuller story, Electa remained reticent, defensive, and protective of her husband.

Given this unexpected turn, I could not resist asking Francis what news he had obtained in his time in the mining town. He confirmed the account he had shared at the farm of Plummer's slaying Cleveland, adding even more terrifying details of Plummer's calculated efforts to eliminate a man who knew his compromised past too well. Francis pointed out Plummer's swollen, misaligned right wrist and disclosed how a bullet had entered the arm at the elbow and lodged in the wrist when the lawman attempted to murder another witness to his crimes. This time the informant had fled to safety far from Bannack.

I found myself studying Plummer with renewed fascination and dread. Those mangled fingers of the left hand first glimpsed at Fort Benton the previous October now took on added meaning, a hieroglyphics of violence, of woe. His abrupt turns in conversation now seemed evasions rather than wit, and his brusque manner to all kinds of men hinted at latent conflict or collusion, one could not tell which. Perhaps most disturbing was Francis's news that Plummer had recently warned him not to trust anyone to enter his store at night unbidden, for many a criminal preyed upon the populace. How could the sheriff know such a thing and yet not stop it?

It was with relief and sorrow, then, that we saw Electa board a coach for Salt Lake City on September 2, 1863, less than three months after her wedding. There was no doubting her fondness for her husband, written in her tearful eyes and trembling embraces. Harvey and Mary implored her to stay, but go she must, and how blessed an event in light of what was to come. If we could truly see the future, we too would have boarded that coach. I know now Henry came to wish he had done so. He accompanied her as far as the Snake River crossing, returning with a despondent face and slumped shoulders.

At first we lived a surprising kind of calm. To confirm his intention to join his wife soon, Plummer sold me his cabin, under the agreement he could board with us. It was a gentlemanly gesture. Henry, Francis, and Joseph continued to take meals with us, while I worked my modest claim, Francis tended to his store, and Plummer played the part of sheriff. Perhaps that is too cruel a way of phrasing the man's actions. I did witness many efforts on his part to keep the peace in that often raucous town. The people respected and liked him; they trusted him. In his genteel way, he could calm a loud drinker, break up an incipient fight, or find missing horses. He genuinely seemed to enjoy the part of peacekeeper, it suited him. I was especially struck by his ready banter with the likes of Granville Stuart, who counted as a long-time resident of the region, having arrived in this country in 1857. Stuart had met Henry on his first arrival in Idaho Territory, and by Granville's telling, he took an instant shine to the soon-to-be sheriff. If a man as well-traveled and sagacious as Stuart could attest to Henry's virtues, how could I doubt them?

Yet outside our circle of calm, something was terribly wrong. Gold had been struck in Alder Gulch to the east, a placer mining site that showed promise of being far more lucrative than Bannack. As gold continued to pour out of these two camps, with lucky strikers eager to take their winnings east by river or road, the number of attacks on lone riders and coaches had jumped. It was not uncommon to hear of murder in isolated places on a weekly basis. Inevitably our eyes turned to Henry, for as sheriff, he seemed strangely unaffected by these crimes. For all his attention to the daily comportment of Bannack citizens, he showed little stomach for investigating and stopping these atrocities. I would casually mention these dire happenings over our meals, but Henry only deflected the issue, arguing that these were random acts in a wide open country with many places for road agents to conceal themselves. No, he would avow, if he could discern a pattern and a conspiracy, he would strike at the head of the cabal.

I leap ahead to Thanksgiving, 1863, because it was the last moment of familial joy, and because in hindsight it was a ghastly masquerade. Bannack was experiencing what folks in this territory call an open winter, with little snowfall and relatively warm days. That weather proved a boon to miners who could work their claims in late November. My wife, ever a fine hostess, invited a party of dignitaries to celebrate the national holiday and the preternaturally generous weather: Judge Sidney Edgerton and his family, Edgerton's nephew Wilbur Sanders and his family, Francis Thompson, Joseph Swift, and, of course, Henry Plummer. The Edgertons and Sanders had arrived earlier this fall, shortly after Electa left. In fact, Plummer had accompanied them to Bannack after separating from his wife at Snake River ferry. Theirs was a curious story, one I continue to ponder: Edgerton had been appointed judge of Idaho Territory, yet rather than journeying to Lewiston west of the Bitterroot Mountains, the seat of the territory, he traveled to Bannack, east of that daunting mountain chain. Edgerton's intelligence and shrewdness were manifest, yet he claimed to have arrived in our town quite by accident. Given his current mission, lobbying for a new territory in the nation's capital, I wonder if it was more than happenstance that brought him to our narrow valley the fall of '63.

Governor Sidney Edgerton. Montana Historical Society Research Center Photograph Archives, Helena, Montana

We were a festive, well-turned party, choosing this occasion to wear our finest garb and sip the best wine available. Henry purchased a forty-pound turkey from Salt Lake City for the dinner, no doubt as much a gesture of politics as conviviality. He knew his future as sheriff and civic leader depended on courting these new citizens, not least because of their contrasting party loyalties, Democrat and Republican. For Martha Jane and me, this was an opportunity to entertain leading lights in this part of Idaho Territory and put behind us a protracted period of gloom. While our faith often sustained us, we were not immune to doubts about the wisdom of our transplanting to the headwaters of the Missouri. There was a reason this isolated, difficult terrain was among the last to be penetrated by Americans—it was not just remote but daunting and dangerous.

Henry played host (why do I always think of him as a thespian?), Martha Jane served the meal, and I poured the wine and assured our guests' comfort. There was a palpable sense of being at the beginning of things, the start of a new country, as though we were the Argonauts who explored the west to lay the foundation for a mighty civilization. Inevitably, as is the wont of people who have traveled far from home and find themselves thrown together by fate, we shared our travel tales. Our journey up the Missouri the spring of '62 took on an epic cast, buffalo and Indians and limestone cliffs that seemed God's cathedral. Animated Sanders took us over the Oregon Trail, then up the Corinne Road, through his vivid rendering in words. He did not conceal the party's surprise and disappointment upon coming over the hill to glimpse Bannack for the first time, the dour cabins and muddy streets in the gloomy canyon. But on this evening, with candles in profusion and spirits rising, that grim memory took on a comic cast. Martha Edgerton told an amusing story on her father, which I wrote down for later recollection:

"Shortly after arriving at Bannack, my father strolled up Main street to see the town. Coming to a building where miners' court was in progress, he went in. The judge, seeing that he was a stranger, invited my father to sit beside him. The trial of the case proceeded, but not for long, when it was interrupted by the suggestion of some one present that it was time liquid refreshments should be served. The judge and everyone present approving of the suggestion, an old darkey was dispatched to a neighboring saloon for the whisky. On his return, the court took a recess and a drink, several of them in fact. When the liquor was exhausted and the court and those in attendance upon it sufficiently stimulated, the trial went on, only to meet with a similar interruption in the course of half an hour or so. This was the initiation of the new Chief Justice into western methods of legal procedure."

Only Henry was curiously reticent about his journey to Bannack, brushing over his time in California and Washington Territory and lavishing our humble farm with praise. It was good to hear him elevate his distant wife, to recount the wedding ceremony just last June, to tell of their honeymoon journey to Bannack. To Henry's credit, he evinced deep emotion when recalling Electa.

Inevitably our free-flowing conversation swirled around the war, for at such a remove from the action we desperately craved news, and it was hard to come by at that time of year when travel was constricted and few newspapers arrived. Condescension and contempt toward the rebels entered Judge Edgerton's words as he told what he knew of Gettysburg and Vicksburg, those signal victories that occurred simultaneously as if by fate or design last July, and of course, Mr. Sanders had served on the Union side in the war. Henry showed impressive tact during this passage in our intercourse, choosing to remain silent rather than debate the national troubles. In truth, Henry's politics always struck me as pliable; though a declared Democrat, he rarely came across as a doctrinaire bore.

Following the turkey and the pie, the gentlemen smoked cigars provided by Plummer, and the ladies withdrew to their part of the cabin to visit. For the first time conversation drifted to the wave of criminality in the region, beginning with a casual mention by Sanders that attacks on travelers seemed to be increasing and the open weather only encouraged more such assaults. Plummer presented himself as the very figure of insouciance, replying that the highwaymen were surely a disparate lot, motivated by private grudges and moments of opportunity to assault isolated stages. When Judge Edgerton begged to differ, observing a seeming coordination in the efforts, Plummer demurred, refusing to take the bait and debate the issue. I now realize this may have been Henry's last chance to save himself from what was about to come. Had he mounted a spirited, credible defense at this very moment, perhaps Sanders might have chosen not to prosecute him. Henry was the kind of man people prefer to believe, even if they sense he is hedging the truth. Charming to the end, he invited leniency. But at this most critical instant, his political and persuasive instincts did not serve him.

Writing this memoir on a blustery May day, with full knowledge that Martha Jane and I must soon depart this farm and return to Iowa, I relish the memory of that last good evening with Plummer. Yet I find myself wondering whether he sensed his guests were probing him, testing him, seeking to understand his part in the carnival of crime. If so, Henry never evidenced nervousness or doubt. He had weathered a hard life, survived many scrapes, and lived to suppress the tale. No doubt he believed he would survive this close brush with self-righteous men determined to make a mark on this unformed region. In the end his charm failed him.

Shortly after our Thanksgiving feast, Gad Upson, the new Indian agent to the Blackfeet, replacing our minister Reed, arrived in Bannack on his way to claim his position at Benton City. Given the unreliability of the Missouri waters, he had chosen the overland route along the Corinne Road. He was a bumptious, confident man, full of opinions. He was especially critical of the management of the government farm, as he called it, asking whether I might consider returning as caretaker. He was uncertain of the current condition of the fort but he had heard good reports of my service there. To Upson's credit, he was determined to resuscitate the farm, though for reasons I could not fully credit: He believed the Indians pure savages in need of steady instruction in civilization. And so it was that I contracted to take up my duties at the farm once again, in the middle of that strangely moderate winter. It would mean separation from Martha Jane and the children, but I assumed it would be temporary, for they would join me once spring arrived in full force in the mountain fastness. Of course, we also assumed Henry would be departing for Iowa and we would have no further reason to stay in Bannack.

And so it was that I once again followed the Madison River north to our old home on the Sun River in late December, the weather turning cold and bitter. For the first time I learned my successor had been one Malcolm Clarke, who had secured appointment as resident farmer in our absence. By Upson's account, Clarke had turned the fort into a kind of prairie trading post and brothel for travelers along the Mullan. I could hardly credit Upson's words, yet Clarke was familiar to me through legend: He was an original American Fur Company factor, a tall, violent-tempered man married to a Piegan wife, with many offspring from their union. Rumor had it he had killed many a man, Indian and white, who crossed him. He was not a man to be toyed with. Clarke had already decamped, however, following a confrontation with the new Indian agent, and an obscure man with an elusive past served as temporary caretaker.

Our horses and cattle looked none the better for wear; all the work we had expended repairing fence and barn had come undone, in part through the hurricane winds that came off the mountain front, in part through human hands that took delight in destroying this emblem of American settlement. Our native

neighbors had once again stripped the farm of most of its implements, no doubt to trade for whiskey. "During the fore part of
the month of January I had no teams to work with, and I busied
myself with repairing the houses, fitting up farming utensils, and
getting wood as best I could. About the middle of the month I
received two span of mules and immediately commenced haul-
ing wood for house use, and logs for building a stock corral,
repairing and removing fences, and clearing the land for culti-
vation. These duties occupied my time until the 1st of March."
    I worked with a heavy heart, for word had arrived of Henry's
hanging. The news reached me first as a rumor along the Mullan, stray travelers telling me of vigilante justice in the camps.
With heart in throat, I asked these sojourners if they had word
of Plummer. They nodded their heads and relayed varying accounts of his end. Why was I not surprised by this news? I wanted to run to Martha Jane, to comfort her, for what a horror it
must have been to witness. At last I caught a glimpse of her riding the government ambulance over the hill nearest the farm,
accompanied by a gentleman returning to Benton to engage in
trade. How she trembled when we embraced, unable to speak
for a time, and then such a story of woe. The Vigilance Committee had been efficient and ruthless, refusing her a chance to
speak to Henry as he approached his death. She said they feared
her presence would break their will. Poor young Swift, who defended Plummer through thick and thin, broke down and wept
outside the ring of vengeance. Sanders, our Thanksgiving guest,
refused to attend the hanging, though rumor had it he instigated
the final verdict, a prosecuting attorney in full.
    Self-recrimination must be the hardest sentence of all. Time
and again Martha Jane and I have revisited our year and a half in
this wind-swept, majestic, but terrible place. So many choices, so
many turning points, so many opportunities to evade this final
fate. Sometimes at night, with our little ones fast asleep, we weep
in each other's arms, thinking, "If only, if only." I take responsi-

bility for the first step to Henry's doom, for had I not sought his protection that October day at Benton City, he might well have returned east, ahead of his shameful demise. Martha Jane sometimes chastises me for these sentiments, avowing our innocence, insisting on all the choices Plummer made for himself. It was a danse macabre, that Thanksgiving feast, as Plummer played the part of the respectable lawman, Edgerton and Sanders the sympathetic citizens. In the end the iron-willed Republicans had their way.

Our hopes for this obscure corner of Idaho Territory are indeed blasted. Electa received word of Plummer's ignominious death by early February, for Martha Jane sent a letter by way of a party taking the Corinne Road south. The news was also transmitted via telegraph from Salt Lake City and taken up by newspapers in the States. We have determined to return to Iowa this autumn, only completing our duties here as best we can. Our faith in God and in each other sustains us. May Henry rest in peace, and may Electa begin life anew. One cannot help wondering if she will ever trust to love again. For now we plan to go east to support her, to remind her that she has a long life to live, and to say over and over her Idaho tragedy need not script the rest of her days. As for Martha Jane and me, we are determined to find a new home in a far more settled place, with an established community and less proximity to the Indians. We remain true to our belief the native people are not inherent savages but souls in need of charity and instruction. Little Dog showed us that with his transient efforts at supporting the farm. But in the end, it will take far more force and persistence than we can muster at this time. God willing, men like Upson, Thompson, and Stuart will make a civilized place of this after all.

MAY IS THE TIME OF THE BITTERROOT, AND SO THE TIME FOR Victor and his people to journey up and down the valley named for this flower, to collect and preserve its edible roots. Salish legend tells that the bitterroot was born one spring when a starving woman's tears were transformed into the saving flower. John Owen observed the harvesting of the bitterroot in 1852, and his journal entries reveal the fullness and complexity of Salish life in their homeland:

> the Indians are removing the Cache of Meat they Made here on the return from Buffaloe & [now are] Making one of Bitter Root[.] Victor the head chief was down & told Me he intended Making a start to Morrow Morning for the Camash [camas] ground Which root I believe is about ready for digging—The Bitter Root is all made & from appearance they had a bountiful harvest.

The Salish seasonal round of acquiring food is revealed, encompassing a buffalo hunt, harvesting the bitter root, and seeking the camas. In other entries made during this period Owen records the easy interchange among nations in the region, including the Blackfeet, Shoshone, and Nez Perce. Times are trying as well, however, since the journal-keeper will note the deaths of several Salish women from disease.

Three years later Victor will be a principal negotiator of the Hellgate, or Council Grove, Treaty, the Americans' transparent effort to claim land for railroad construction and white settlement. Having completed his survey for a path across the Northwest, Washington Governor Isaac Stevens now negotiates terms with various nations to secure a throughway with one purpose: Drive a vector from the upper Midwest to the Pacific Northwest to facilitate migration and nation-building. The back-and-forth between Stevens and chiefs of the Kootenai, Pend d'Oreille, and Salish peoples turns especially difficult when they consider the location of a common reservation. While the Kootenais and Pend d'Oreilles will favor the Jocko valley, their ancestral homeland, Victor insists on holding onto his people's Bitterroot home.

Yet his choices, his challenges are even more complicated than
this summary implies:

> Victor faced probably the most difficult problem of his
> life. He had agreed to the one reservation proposal. He
> knew, on the one hand, that Alexander's people [the Up-
> per Pend d'Oreilles] were loath to leave the Mission and
> might not follow their chief if he agreed to move to the
> Bitterroot Valley. On the other hand, Victor knew that
> his own people were divided in their opinion. Moise,
> the Flathead second chief, was opposed to any land ces-
> sion whatever. Bear Track, the powerful medicine man,
> refused to leave the Bitterroot Valley. Many of his people
> were still hostile to Missions and might refuse to follow
> him if he agreed to move to a reservation near St. Igna-
> tius. His own position as chief was not strong. Should
> he make an unpopular decision, that position might be
> lost. Not only his own future but that of his tribe was at
> stake. Victor refused to be stampeded or shamed into
> a decision.

Victor's qualities as a leader were apparent to Father Pierre-
Jean De Smet, fabled Jesuit missionary, who believed the Salish
warrior was named head chief of his people in 1841 because of
his equanimity, humility, and faith. The Salish leader combined
indigenous and Catholic piety, showing how mixing cultural
practices could yield a good life. Stevens noted Victor's slowness
of speech and seems to have interpreted this rhythm as revealing simplicity of thought. The opposite was surely true. The Salish chief had that rare and powerful ability to remain calm in
a crisis, to slow down conversation and deliberation to assure
full thought and careful consideration. It is precisely those intel-
lectual qualities that allowed him to achieve the best possible
outcome during the Council Grove negotiations. After all, Stevens' demands must have taken Victor by surprise. Rather than

limiting discussions to preventing the Blackfeet from stealing horses and killing Flathead warriors, Stevens was insisting on land concessions. It was Victor's challenge to find a middle way to forestall disaster for his people. The Salish chief will resolve the dilemma of the reservation's location through skillful ambiguity. In the words of the Hellgate Treaty's Article 11:

> It is, moreover, provided that the Bitter Root Valley, above the Loo-lo Fork, shall be carefully surveyed and examined, and if it shall prove, in the judgment of the President, to be better adapted to the wants of the Flathead tribe than the general reservation provided for in this treaty, then such portions of it as may be necessary shall be set apart as a separate reservation for the said tribe. No portion of the Bitter Root Valley, above the Loo-lo Fork, shall be opened to settlement until such examination is had and the decision of the President made known.

Victor has prevented the interlopers from removing his people by insisting on hedging language that at the very least defers a day of reckoning. It will not be until President Grant's 1871 decree that the Flathead Salish will be told to move north to the Jocko Valley, and even then, Victor's son Charlo will resist removal until 1891.

ABRAHAM LINCOLN STANDS WITH PEN IN HAND, REFLECTIVE. How many changes he and his Republican Congress have effected during three years of war: the Homestead Act and the creation of new territories out west, the land of gold, as many call it, a source of bullion and hope. Even as the seceshes seek to rend the United States, the country continues to expand with new territories that tell the world this experiment in democratic government is enduring and vital. Fair to say Sidney Edgerton, an old friend, was the key to getting this document before the

Victor, Chief of the Salish, ca. 1864. RAVALLI COUNTY MUSEUM AR-
CHIVES, HAMILTON, MONTANA

tall man, his passion, persistence, and displays of gold nuggets assuring passage. Edgerton had visited just a few days before, readying for return to his far western home. He mentioned he heard rumors that a senator had lodged an objection to his being named first territorial governor. When the tall man confirmed the rumor, Edgerton replied he was agreeable to whatever course the tall man would follow, sharing the observation, "I should return home and mine as Dosheimer kept tavern." "Dosheimer, I knew Dosheimer. What was the story?" the president replied. The story was this: "Dosheimer attended a convention at Utica hoping to obtain the nomination as Canal Commissioner. He was defeated, and rising from his seat, said, 'Shentleman, I goes back to Puffalo and keeps tavern like hell.'" The tall man laughed heartily at the story.

Lincoln meditates briefly on the speed with which the Northwest, so long a *terra incognita*, claimed by Russia, Spain, Great Britain, and the United States, has become parceled out into these new political units, adolescents on their way to full adulthood, territories incubating states. Just last March he had signed the bill creating Idaho Territory, and now this new entity. Oh well, he trusts Edgerton as an honorable, decent man, and a stout Republican, and he fears what might become of that isolated outpost of Idaho should the seceshes continue emigrating there.

Crafting the Organic Act has exposed fault lines on the question of Negro suffrage, leading to tortured debate and delays in passage. Lincoln's reelection may hinge on these very questions. At one point Senator Wilkinson of Minnesota, a key ally, had stood on the floor to proclaim,

> There are some Negroes there.…I wish to state that I called upon a friend of mine who has moved into Montana from St. Paul, Minnesota, and I asked him that question. He replied that there were Negroes there; that one

of the most respectable men in the Territory was a Negro worth over fifty thousand dollars.

That friend was of course Nathaniel Langford. But as it happened, Langford had told a tall tale, and Senator Wilkinson felt betrayed when his friend from St. Paul insisted that no such Negroes existed in the soon-to-be territory, relieving senators from the burden of legislating for actual beings on the ground.

In the end, Congress used a legislative sleight of hand to protect white male voting privileges, signaling just how difficult it would be to enfranchise freedmen. That dust-up would also lead Wilkinson to lodge the formal objection to Edgerton's serving as first territorial governor.

Even settling on a suitable name for this new political entity involves sometimes playful, sometimes hateful suggestions. The Democrats push for the names Jefferson or Douglas, in honor of the party's founder and one of the tall man's chief antagonists, Stephen Douglas. When Shoshone is suggested, in an attempt to provide a proper Indian gloss, it is observed that this tribe's name translated as "snake," which could be interpreted as a sly endorsement of Copperhead sympathy for the Confederate cause. And then there is the sarcastic proposal to name the new territory "Abysinnia," reference to Republican commitment to African American rights.

Fortunately, in their wisdom, Congress settles on the name "Montana," which translates as "mountain" in Spanish and Latin and has the added virtue of echoing the name for this vast region attributed to Indians, "The Land of Shining Mountains." These toxic debates only reinforce the struggle over the nation's future political arrangements, and demonstrate how the contest between the Unionists and Rebels is seeping into every corner of the vast continent, even this seemingly distant, wild place. Yes, to forestall some extension of that Southern fantasy of a new nation, the president must assure that land is fully incorporated into these United States.

And so on this 26th day of May, 1864, Abraham Lincoln signs the bill creating the Territory of Montana.

JUNE

In which Abram Voorhees journeys to and from Montana and summer comes to the Assiniboine.

_____

*June is the Moon of Hatching, most birds eggs hatch. It is also
the Moon of High Waters, the moon when the sarvis berry, or
serviceberry, begins to ripen.*

_____

❝ [T]HE EXPENSES TOIL & PRIVATIONS INCIDENT TO A TRIP TO the mining region are not justified by the real condition of things there." So concludes Abram Voorhees, a forty-year-old farmer from Michigan who helps lead a train of emigrants along the Bozeman Trail—in fact, the first train—in 1864. In his detailed record of the trip, Voorhees comes across as the still point in a turning world, a calm, stable center around which swirl wild desire, cross purposes, strained relationships, fear of Indian predation, physical pain, and stark disappointments. This sober rendering of the boom reminds time and again that there were few winners and many losers in the flush times of early Montana.

Having formed a company with fellow Michiganders, a practice common among sojourners to the remote northwest as a hedge against financial loss, Voorhees hitched his literal and proverbial wagons to one Allen Hurlbut, preparing to lead a caravan of wagons along the Powder River route first attempted by John Bozeman the previous summer. Hurlbut had at least two compelling attractions: He seemed to know his way around this wild, unfamiliar country, and he promised to show travelers the means to golden wealth in the Big Horn River country, far east of the diggings in southwestern Montana and so potentially far more lucrative. This second promise would prove the undoing of Hurlbut's command.

Voorhees' motives for taking such a risk at his advanced stage of life will remain forever unknown. He was the most affluent member of his Michigan company and so would seem to have the most to lose by the trek. He shows little interest in prospecting during the expedition, preferring instead to hunt, fish, and enjoy his idle time in camp. His descriptions of the terrain they cross are usually utilitarian, functional, and so he does not strike the reader as a student of landscapes or pictorial effects. And most telling of all, once the train reaches Virginia City, he takes only five days to determine he will return home, and so promptly reverses course to his Michigan farm. One might speculate that he accompanied his partners as a kind of mentor or protector, or perhaps even this sober-sides was swept up in the frenzy of Idaho (soon to be Montana) gold, drawn into the vortex of greed, ambition, and hope.

Hurlbut's train would have the honor of beating Bozeman to the trail in June 1864, but Bozeman would pass him en route and so claim priority in completing the journey for the first time. It was a large, even imposing gathering of emigrants, wagons, and animals:

> when we left the main road we numbered 124 wagons 112 horses 68 mules 392 oxen 70 cows 418 men 10 women 10 children 2092 gun & pistol shots & 20 dogs.

The train's scale probably explains one of the central mysteries of their fairly uneventful journey: Why didn't the Sioux and Cheyenne intercept and discourage this clear violation of prime hunting grounds, as they had the year before in stopping

Abram Voorhees. Yale Collection of Western Americana, Beinecke Rare Book and Manuscript Library, Yale University, New Haven, Connecticut

Bozeman's first, much smaller expedition? Voorhees notes many signs of Indian presence along the trail, such as coming upon just-abandoned camp sites and finding materials or wounded dogs left behind. Surely the allied tribes were well aware of this loud, cumbersome, strung out, invasive force. Leaders and warriors must have concluded the party was too large to take on with a direct challenge. They may have also believed—hoped—Hurlbut's and Bozeman's trains would be the only two of the season. Perhaps that explains why the third such expedition—A.A. Townsend's—would be attacked, leading to the death of four emigrants.

Voorhees was one of the leaders of this large force, serving as marshal during the first half of the expedition. He shows a meticulous eye for the condition of animals and wagons, the quality of water available, the amount of forage and shade. He also observes with telling objectivity the mood among the emigrants as they advance up a trail already marked by Indian presence. As a keen farmer he notes, for example, that Indians had cut down cottonwood branches along the river to browse their ponies during the previous winter. The company also finds the remains of emigrants who are rumored to have encountered a Crow party the summer before (these would have been the men lost in James Stuart's first expedition to the Big Horn in '63).

But above all, Voorhees is sensitive to shifting moods among men with diverging motives, crossed desires. Since Hurlbut had assured members of the train he knew how to find gold in the Big Horn country, emigrants grow increasingly restless with futility when that promise does not pan out. A journal entry for July 13th, almost a month on the trail, reads as placid, even pastoral:

> we are in camp near 3 miles from where the river comes
> out of the mountain a number of men are out prospect-
> ing others are fishing the others are laying in the shade

& there is need of shade for the captains [Hurlbut's]
thermometer stands 135 in sunshine & 102 in the shade
I gathered a dish of wild currants here & Cub caught a
mess of fish we had good swim in big horn to day.

Yet a serpent lurks in this garden, for just four days later,
Voorhees records,

they say they think there is gold on [the] head waters
of this river but we are on the wrong side of the mountain....there is not much good feeling towards the captain
[Allen Hurlbut] at this time he has deceived us to[o]
much.

And with that almost understated entry, Voorhees sets the
stage for a surprising turn of events: Many emigrants choose to
form their own train, cutting Hurlbut out as leader and turning
to Voorhees as commander of the newly formed party. Reading
between the lines of the new commander's spare prose, a contemporary reader senses the emigrants' impatience, exhaustion,
pain, fear, and homesickness. They are crossing terrain known
to them only by rumor and guidebooks such as J.L. Campbell's
Idaho: Six Months in the New Gold Diggings that prove wildly
inaccurate; they must trust guides unknown to them, gauging
the leaders' abilities in the moment, on the road; they know the
threat of Indian attack, and they bear witness to the ominous
remains of that violence; they come tantalizingly close to a big
strike, finding good color, only to realize the source is beyond
their reach, on the other side of a massive mountain range; and
the heat of summer on the plains is unbearable. No wonder the
train fractures, comes apart.

Voorhees' voice changes subtly as he takes command of this
new party. He becomes a bit more expansive and descriptive.
Perhaps the change is due to their moving into the Yellowstone
River basin, a terrain lush by comparison with the Powder and

Big Horn rivers country they have left behind. Perhaps much of
the tension surrounding Hurlbut's fraught leadership has been
drained away, allowing the Michigan man to expound more
fully on travelers and their surroundings. In a remarkable encounter along the Stillwater River, a tributary of the Yellowstone,
Voorhees meets the mighty Jim Bridger, an occasion that yields
a comic description and a sobering statement about the gold
boom:

> while stoping here captain Bridger [Jim Bridger] came
> along in a buggy drawn by two mules he is a tough look-
> ing old chap there were a number of wagons both freight
> and returning emigrants with him we saw them coming
> & thought it was a chance to send some letters home
> we pitched in & wrote a few & some of his party carried
> them off with them they tell a mournful tale of the mines
> & that men are leaving for home as fast as they come.

Having completed his first expedition along his cut-off, the
seasoned guide leads a return party to the Platte River, where
he will form the very train that John Owen describes in his
salty journal from September and October. If it is tempting to
see Bridger as the six-foot-tall, clear-eyed, tireless wilderness
sage, the image of him in a buggy pulled by two mules dis-
courages such mythologizing. Voorhees also reminds us that
Old Gabe was indeed old, sixty to be precise, in the year of
Montana's creation.

More telling than the amusingly disrespectful description
of the captain is recognition of the futility suffered by so many
Argonauts. In Voorhees' dry prose, the word "mournful" rings
with unusual resonance. It is likely the train's leader had already
begun to anticipate his own hasty retreat from the alien and
alienating landscapes of the high plains and northern Rockies,
so that telling adjective communicates as much about his state
of mind as that of the emigrants he meets under Bridger's com-

mand. But the word suggests a dirge-like death of dreams, a final recognition of the limits of American longing, the sense of another chance played out, a sad epilogue to a desperate flight toward possibility. It is the story too often suppressed, even repressed, in most contemporary and later accounts of the boom. Mention of letters to be carried toward home hint at one of the underlying causes of this elegy in a Montana river basin: the desperate longing for a familiar place, familiar faces, familiar habits and gestures. At times the gold rush causes emigrants to take on habits, to act in ways that seem uncanny, malformed, misplaced, even inhuman. Perhaps this distorting environment begins to explain the violence of the early boom days, violence registered in the casual murder of Indians and whites alike, the focused fury of the vigilance committee, the indifference to humans lost to death along the trail.

VOORHEES' PARTY HAS TWO CLOSE ENCOUNTERS WITH NATIVE peoples, incidents suggesting the ambiguity, even confusion surrounding the emigrants' relations with the nations. Shortly after the break with Hurlbut, Indians of an unidentified tribe run off with livestock poorly attended by the emigrants:

> & here the horsemen were careless & had been before & while the cattle had guards with them the horses were looked after from their tents if looked after at all & just as we were eating our breakfast the Indians about 20 or 25 of them were seen among the horses that were a mile away from the camp[. M]en with their rifles were after them horses running in every direction trying to get to camp & some were lucky enough to reach it one mule came in with an arrow sticking in its side while 6 horses & 6 mules were driven off by them before our men could [get] near to them there were a good many shots fired at them but none were killed.

The incident suggests the crossed lines of communication, authority, and responsibility that would inevitably follow from an abrupt change in leadership. This is one of the few moments in the journal when Voorhees protects himself from censure through a rhetorical trick, prefacing the description of the raid with reference to previous occasions of the guards' carelessness, as though this debacle did not fall at the new leader's feet.

By contrast, just nine days later, an encounter with the Crows along the Yellowstone yields a moment of rapport and ease:

> we camped just below an Indian camp that was on opposite side of the river from us soon after we camped there were three came to our tents one of them was the son of the chief of the Crows he appeared to be very friendly & a good natured fellow they had good ponies in fact they were the best we had seen on the trip soon after there were 4 more come 2 were squaws we gave them some bread & meat.

When the train crosses the divide into the Missouri River drainage, the journalist's voice takes on another cast altogether, for he has entered a region of rich farmland that brings out an enthusiasm, even eagerness missing in his earlier descriptions. The Gallatin River Valley impresses him as ideal farm country, and he notes many farms already under operation. Since Voorhees passes through the valley just days before the founding of Bozeman City, his acute appreciation for the agricultural possibilities takes on added meaning. A successful farmer from the upper Midwest is bearing witness to the potential of this land recently claimed by white settlers. In a poignant passage, evocative of the farmer-writer's longings, Voorhees records with special clarity this welcome spectacle along the road from East Gallatin to Virginia City:

near here we passed the first house since leaving the Platt
it was built of small logs or poles covered with the same
and dirt thrown on the poles they were putting up hay at
this ranche at noon we stoped on willow creek in afternoon we passed several ranches & at night we camped on
meadow brook near Newmans ranche it is the first time
we heard the sound of a reaper.

This transparent fondness for the yeoman's life prepares the
reader for the anticlimactic conclusion to Voorhees' sojourn to
the far west:

& now we are in Virginia City after a long journey &
where we did not expect to go when leaving the Platt but
not finding that for which we sought on the way we have
kept looking up to here & find the prospect rather small
here.

VOORHEES HAS FULFILLED HIS DUTY TO THE EMIGRANTS WHO
chose him as leader of their party, going far beyond the Big
Horn country that had been his—and their—original destination. Underwhelmed by opportunity in the most wide-open
of Montana mining towns, he divides the goods and livestock
with his partners and beats a hasty retreat for home within five
days of arriving in Alder Gulch. He expresses no sentimentality
for this far-off boom town—the decision to turn homeward is
easy and practical. Pragmatic to the end, though betraying more
emotion than he might suppose in his Spartan prose, Abram
Voorhees gladly brings to an end one of the great adventures of
his life, an adventure that failed to yield the payoff for which he
must have hoped.

Assiniboine legend teaches:

Towards morning, before the light showed and when slumber was in every lodge, the Lynx softly walked to the yellow lodge and looked in. The four old men were all asleep. The bag, containing the summer, was hanging on the tripod in the back part of the lodge.

The summer was in the form of spring water. It moved about in a bag made from the stomach of a buffalo. Now and then it overflowed and trickled along the ground, under the tripod, and in its wake green grass and many different kinds of plants and flowers grew luxuriantly.

Cautiously, on stealthy feet, the Lynx entered, stepping over the entrance and, with a quick jerk, snapped the cord that held the bag. Seizing it tightly in his teeth, he plunged through the door and sped away.

Almost the same instant the old men awakened and gave the alarm: "The summer has been stolen!" The cry went from lodge to lodge and in a short time a group on fast horses were after the Lynx.

They were fast gaining on the Lynx when he gave the bag to the Red Fox who was waiting. The horsemen then killed the Lynx and started after the Fox who, after a time, gave the bag to the Antelope. The Antelope took it to the Coyote, who brought it to the Wolf, the long-winded one, who was to deliver it to the waiting party. Each time the bag was passed to the next runner, the winded animal was killed by the pursuers.

The fast horses were tired but gained steadily on the Wolf. As he sped across the country, the snow melted away directly behind him; the grass sprang up green; trees and bushes unfolded their leaves as the summer passed by. Fowls seemed to join the pursuit, as flock after flock flew northward.

As the Wolf crossed the river the ice moved and broke up. By the time the horsemen reached it, the river was flowing bank-full of ice. This halted the Southern people. In sign language they said to the Assiniboine, "Let us bargain with each other for the possession of the summer." After a time it was decided that each would keep the summer for six moons. Then it was to be taken back to the river and delivered to the waiting party.

That agreement was kept, so there was summer half of the year in each country. In that way there were the two seasons, the winter and the summer.

General Alfred Sully. Montana Historical Society Research Center Photograph Archives, Helena, Montana

JULY

In which General Sully leads an attack on the Hunkpapa Sioux and their allies, street fights break out in Benton City on the Fourth of July, a Protestant minister arrives on the Madison River, and Last Chance Gulch is discovered.

July is the Moon of Ripe Berries, the gathering of the holy encampment that comes annually, midsummer time.

GENERAL ALFRED SULLY IS DISTRACTED, IRRITABLE— contending forces battle in his mind. While preparing to strike the Hunkpapa Sioux and their allies the Blackfoot Lakota, Santees, Yankonais, Sans Arcs, and Miniconjous in western Dakota, he wrestles with the fate of Minnesotans following the Northern Overland Route to the Montana mines. He writes to his commanding officer from Fort Rice, at the junction of the Cannonball and Missouri rivers:

> A large body of emigrant wagons and ox-teams and with women and children have followed the Minnesota troops to this point....I wish they were away from here. I can't send them back. I can't leave them here, for I can't feed them, and they even have come to me for permission to purchase rations, which I cannot do, for there is danger of my not getting enough rations up here to supply the post on account of low water, and the river is falling rapidly.

How can Sully protect the Minnesotans while punishing the hostiles? His large but unwieldy force will become disoriented in a wilderness of badlands and plains and elusive enemies. It will become a forced march through hell, or as Sully puts it, "Hell, with the fires out." There will be no battlefield flourishes or frontal assaults such as he knew under the command of General McClellan in Virginia during the early days of the War of the Rebellion. No, in this broken, vile country, on which wagon wheels shatter and horses die from heat and thirst, it will be hit and miss for both native and soldier. It becomes an extended skirmish, fire and duck, as his 800 wagons relentlessly progress toward the massed Indian camp near Killdeer Mountain. The Sioux do not hide— they do not seek to hide—their presence, their knowledge of Sully's pitiless advance. They occasionally send trial arrows or bullets into the train, harass scouts, steal a horse when left unattended. It's their means of giving fair warning, of signaling that they will fight and destroy this massed army of 2,200 soldiers. They are not afraid.

Though Sully is probably not aware of it at the time, two of the most famous Sioux leaders of all, Sitting Bull and Gall, help mount this resistance, using tactics that have served them well in previous encounters with these stiff forces that prefer to move in a straight line in a country made for improvisation and guile. In an ironic twist, General Sully has nothing but respect for the Sioux. He considers them the proudest, bravest, most determined Indian fighters on the high plains. He will soon go on record with the federal government declaring this very sentiment, stressing that the Sioux had the good sense not to accept annuities promised by treaty since that dependency leads to emasculated, weak people. Sully will share these views in public because he will be called to account for the very actions his men are about to take, here on the bitter terrain of western Dakota.

Sitting Bull, ca. 1885. LIBRARY OF CONGRESS

Despite the Indians' harassment, intimidation, and boasts, on July 28 Sully's troops approach the main camp, containing 1,600 lodges, with perhaps as many as 1,600 warriors. (Sully estimates 5,000 fighters, but that is surely an exaggeration.) This midsummer encampment, secure at the base of a mountain, is ideal for warm weather habitation, the flowing stream providing water, the lush, almost alpine terrain full of wildlife for game, the backing cliffs providing shelter for the people from the vicious thunderstorms that can shatter a summer afternoon. However, this seemingly secure fortress will not deter Sully from executing his desired tactic: deploy his howitzers to send a devastating fire into the village. Sully has learned the power of cannon during his tour in Virginia. He also believes the broken terrain favors his men's far more accurate long-range rifles and their bayonet charges rather than the natives' preferred method of dashing charges and quick retreats with bows and arrows and aging muskets.

His troops respond well to their commander, despite the fact he is so ill with dysentery that he must be carried in a wagon rather than proudly ride his own mount. They sense his determination to be finished with this business of fighting the resourceful but doomed tribes of the plains country. After a frustrating series of indecisive battles the summer before, with these very hostiles, Sully will not stop until he has delivered the devastating blow, the one that will end the folly of native pride, that will assure safe passage for these emigrants, many of whom he despises because he believes they are deserters from their duty to country by avoiding service in the Union army. In another irony, the general has more respect for his enemy than for the people he has been compelled to protect.

After initial skirmishing on the margins of the camp, the cannons roar in terrible discord and kill as many as 100 natives in rapid order. The soldiers move in to kill any survivors and capture the camp. They will ultimately claim 500 natives slain, a

high number by the standards of Plains warfare. Given the narrow confines of the combat, the number of warriors involved,
and the fury of the fighting, it may be have seemed that high
to the invaders. A more accurate count is probably 150 killed.
Sully personally orders three slain Sioux decapitated and their
heads displayed in revenge for the death of his aide-de-camp.
Savagery flows under many skins. Sully's troops discover that
many of the women, children, and older Sioux had decamped
just ahead of the assault, though it was anything but an orderly
retreat, the Sioux leaders overestimating their ability to stop
the advance: "Children cried, the dogs were under everybody's
feet, mules balked, and pack-horses took fright at the shell-
fire or snorted at the drifting smoke behind them." No matter.
Sully will continue to pursue them all the way to the Yellowstone River—he never wants to bring an armed force into this
god-forsaken place again.

When the smoke clears, Sully orders his men to occupy the
Indian camp for the night, a means of humiliating the warriors
who have managed to avoid death but not the shock of loss. The
men enjoy their one night in this native place, eating the best
meat and drinking the best water they have known or will know
for many days. It is a victory dance, one nation triumphing over
another, a surge of pride in the crater of desired annihilation.
In the morning, they burn everything, the black smoke signaling the death of hope for their enemy. The strategy is simple:
Destroy all the food and hides the Indians had gathered for the
coming winter, and so make it impossible for them to survive
independent of federal aid, and further, make it impossible for
them to put up armed resistance the following spring and summer, a time no doubt of even greater emigration to the Montana
mines. For spite, the soldiers shoot the camp dogs.

Having destroyed native food stuffs in his act of vengeance,
Sully realizes he is low on supplies to feed his men and those
damned emigrants, and so he considers returning east to resup-

ply. But he has only six days' provisions left, making it impossible to retrace his steps and keep his command together. No,
he must push on for the Yellowstone, per the original plan—he
will cut rations, leave animals and supplies behind, but by God,
he will hit those fleeing Sioux and he will rendezvous with the
steamboats on the Yellowstone that carry the supplies he needs.
His goal is to establish a fort at the mouth of the Powder River,
the very place many of these hostiles had spent the previous
winter, in order to put a stop to their horse stealing, depredations, and resistance to the flow of Americans. That fort would
serve as a supply point and source of protection for a new route
along the Yellowstone River toward the Montana mines.

And now the hunters become the hunted, the military expedition and emigrant train strung out and vulnerable in the
badlands of the Little Missouri River. The Sioux, smarting from
their defeat and fearful of conceding victory to this remorseless
enemy, hit the troops sporadically, at unexpected times, in surprising places, to harass the would-be strikers and discourage
them from mounting direct, organized assaults. The Indians are
aided by the broken, desiccated, unyielding terrain. Not only are
wagons and cannon poorly suited to this uneven land, but the
lack of drinkable water and decent grass weakens soldiers and
livestock. The Sioux often rain down arrows on the interlopers
from the bluffs. Though these intermittent attacks take few lives,
they drain the Americans of confidence and a desire for another
try at a pitched battle. Sully orders his band to strike up the music to encourage his demoralized soldiers and demonstrate his
resolve to the enemy, though the strains probably have the opposite effect. Yes, the march through hell goes on, the badlands
sucking the moisture, the very life out of these interlopers, so
unfamiliar with survival in this land, so stiff and unyielding and
incapable. Their mouths become so dry, their tongues so swollen, they cannot speak.

At last, striking the Yellowstone River in newly made Montana Territory, the general allows his men to break ranks and discipline and race for the river to bathe and gulp and shout with relief. His troops are further buoyed by the sight of two small steamboats Sully has commandeered for the expedition, the *Chippewa Falls* and the *Alone*. But the general cannot hide his disappointment at a missing third steamer, for the ruined riverboat carried the corn most essential for feeding his animals. That loss means he must abandon his design to build a fort at the junction of the Powder and the Yellowstone. The projected emigrant route along the Yellowstone Valley will not be realized.

Sully's expedition will take yet another ironic turn: Emigrants and absconding soldiers steal key supplies and head west for the mines. The theft only confirms the general's disdain for men unwilling to take up arms in defense of their country in its hour of sorest need. That depletion will also make it impossible for Sully to sustain the attack he wants so urgently to make final and complete. The general concludes there will be no follow-on assault in this *terra incognita*. He can only hope his show of force will mean the end of Sioux resistance in western Dakota and eastern Montana. It is a fond hope. Instead, he orders his men to march north to Fort Union, a journey that will carry special horrors of its own since they must twice cross the river, causing several men who had barely survived the bone-dry wilderness to drown in the water they had so desperately desired.

Postscript: Sully's time in Montana does not end with his march through the heart of Sioux country to the Yellowstone River. Serving as Montana Superintendent of Indian Affairs, Sully will attempt to intervene to prevent what came to be known as the Marias Massacre, General Baker's attack on a peaceful Piegan camp on January 23, 1870. To forestall such an assault, Sully will call Piegan chiefs to counsel, making a list of demands that, if met, would perhaps stop the drumbeat toward a massive overreaction to Malcolm Clarke's death at the hands of Owl Child.

Sully's efforts will prove futile, and his reward will be the eternal enmity of Phil Sheridan and William Tecumseh Sherman, Civil War heroes and commanders of western troops. He is effectively banished to bureaucratic posts for the rest of his career. Sully dies a bitter man at the age of fifty-six.

I SHALL NEVER FORGET THE FOURTH OF JULY IN BENTON. Most of the men were from the Southern army and their hatred of the North expressed itself in an unmistakable way.

There were 1,500 men in Benton at that time and I saw such desperate characters as the James brothers among them. You can imagine the fights and rows that went on that day. With feelings of mutual hate, inflamed by bad whisky, the men of the North and South were only too eager to come to blows. It was hell upon earth for a time.

So records William Gladstone, former Hudson Bay carpenter, describing the celebration of the United States' birthday in Fort Benton. And so it is that the day set aside to honor a nation's founding becomes the flashpoint for street battles over the very existence of that country.

Benton City is the ideal setting for this clash of beliefs. It is the focal point for travel in and out of the territory during the high season of upper Missouri transportation. No other place so perfectly embodies the frenzy of empire as the U.S.'s innermost port. Not only do riverboats strain to reach this destination to deliver supplies and emigrants, but also the Mullan Road originates here, serving as the primary lifeline to the gold camps fully established in Gold Creek, Bannack, and Virginia City and those about to emerge in places like Last Chance Gulch and Confederate Gulch. Men and materials flow through here at a remarkable pace. And the graft and greed are a wonder to behold. Skimming off goods from Indian annuities has become a way of life, even

North East View, Fort Benton, 1869. This sketch was published in Forest and Stream *April 13, 1907 with the notation "sketch by army officer," shows steamboats and old fort.* MONTANA HISTORICAL SOCIETY RESEARCH CENTER PHOTOGRAPH ARCHIVES, HELENA, MONTANA

for such an estimable business as the American Fur Company. The sheer exhaustion and anxiety of all this seeking after gain means men are wound tight, on a hair trigger, impatient and importunate. One citizen reports that a drunk man who insults a woman is shot down in the street and nothing much is said or done about it. The simple verdict: "That's the way to fix that sort."

Benton, named for Missouri Senator Thomas Hart Benton, that ardent advocate for western expansion, consists of an adobe fort of long standing and

> "a dozen uncouth houses"—dwellings, stores, ware-
> houses, and saloons—strung along a single main street
> facing the river. Miners, drovers, fur traders, and Indian
> women crowded the community; disregarded what little
> law existed; drank and brawled, and sometimes killed,
> with equal facility; and overcharged new arrivals for ev-
> erything from horses to "lemonade made with syrup, at
> thirty-eight cents a glass."

One witness shares the advice, "As to this Fort…we…say to strangers, the less you have to do with it the better." Fort Benton is a relatively new port on the upper Missouri, established just eighteen years earlier as the successor to Fort Mackenzie a few miles downriver at the mouth of the Marias River. The post of Benton was first conceived and built as an outpost of the American Fur Company's ambitious plans to dominate that still-lucrative trade. By 1864, however, the fur business is in steep decline, causing AFC to retreat from its old fort. If anything, Benton takes on added importance following the transition from fur to gold in the region. Three quarters of mining emigrants to south-western Montana pass through this river town, along with all the supplies needed to sustain the boom.

Meanwhile, gold flows out of Montana to the States primarily by this route, as much as two hundred tons between 1862 and

1869, making it a lively scene for thieves, confidence men, and proprietors of liquor and supplies to ease the journey downriver. Steamboats, the primary means to defeat the Missouri's winding, shallow, snagged course, first reached this point in 1860, and the arrival of those crucial suppliers would be hit-and-miss for the remainder of the gold rush years. Frequently supplies and people would be unloaded at Cow Island, a full 200 miles east, before being transported by ox or mule trains to Benton. And of course the fort serves as the seat for the Blackfeet agent, who will distribute annuities to allied Blackfeet nations in September of this very year.

Predictably, then, on the nation's birthday in 1864, this remote port becomes the gathering place for all the violence and dissent circulating in the United States at large as the Civil War moves toward its inevitable conclusion. While all sojourners to the upper Missouri might share a common call to seeking the main chance in the wide open gold rush, they often hold diametrically opposed visions for the nation they would inhabit. Politics is not a casual part of their conversations and jokes, it is the very lifeblood, the skin and bone, of their existence. The long build-up toward civil war meant that young men and women for generations had carried specific and exclusionary understandings of the American experiment. The Mason-Dixon Line ran through their minds and hearts. The dream of a Southern nation was not some fleeting image considered somehow provisional and replaceable. It offered the very purpose for life.

And what is that dream? The North and the South comprise antagonistic, incompatible civilizations. The Southern nation was founded by wise ancestors on the incontrovertible universal law of the superiority of the white race and the inferiority of the Negro race. Jefferson Davis himself described slavery as the means by which "a superior race" transformed "brutal savages into docile, intelligent, and civilized agricultural laborers." The election of Abraham Lincoln meant that Black Republicans had

seized control of the United States government and were determined to subvert the Constitution's guaranteeing slaveholders'
and states' rights. Worse than that, Black Republicans would
incite slaves to rise up in armed rebellion to destroy the very
culture these northerners consider immoral and unjustified.
The women and children of the south would be threatened by
murder, mayhem, and amalgamation. Southern white manhood
could not tolerate this possibility. As one apocalyptic defender
of secession stated the case,

> [Mississippi] had rather see the last of her race, men,
> women and children, immolated in one common funeral
> pile [pyre], than see them subjected to the degradation of
> civil, political and social equality with the negro race.

What was more, the slave states had every right to secede
and form a more perfect union of their own. This was a right
guaranteed by the United States Constitution and universal law.
This new nation would follow the very principles enunciated
in the Declaration of Independence by one of the South's own
great leaders, Thomas Jefferson, throwing off the shackles of
tyranny and establishing a government founded on the consent
of the governed. Radical Republicans' insistence on imposing
abolitionist fanaticism on the entire nation—including those
new territories that would determine the future direction of the
United States—meant that the southern states had no choice
but to break the civil charter and start anew in a confederacy
of states bound by common tradition, common values. And so
it would be that when war came, Southerners and their sympathizers would name it the War of Northern Aggression, for
in their eyes, it was nothing less than an attempt by a diseased
civilization to impose its corrupt institutions and values on an
incompatible, virtuous civilization.

With this dream of a Southern nation firmly planted in the
believers' minds, politics became deeply personal and familial.

They were lived in gestures of disdain, dismissal, and conde-scension. They were lived in a cousin's decision to fight on one side rather than another. They were lived in the very flags people chose to fly on national holidays. But above all, for the many refugees from Missouri, that battle-ground state, that vortex of violence, this clash of civilizations was lived in blood and flesh. Many of the men who found their way to Montana Territory in the dying days of the great national strife lived through guerilla warfare of a savagery difficult to imagine. It all began with the Nebraska-Kansas Act of 1854 and the mad belief that citizens of those new territories could choose their own path toward slav-ery or freedom.

In the incendiary 1850s, in a nation riven by beliefs held with religious intensity, creeds both theological and social, represen-tatives of those competing ways of life would pour into what they considered a *tabula rasa* (with little regard for the native inhab-itants, save to fear and resent them), strive to write their scripts on the landscape of the wide open prairies, assure the extension and survival of their cherished cultures. And it would not be the kindest and gentlest of souls, no, it would be monomaniacs called by their gods to take up arms, to strike down the infidels, to slaughter the detractors and the naysayers. The killing proved intimate and awful. John Brown and his boys became the living symbol of abolitionist fanaticism by massacring a family of pro-slavery people at Pottawatomie, Kansas, with swords, hacking the living, breathing beings to death for the sin of believing one race had the moral right to own another. But that madness only served as prelude to the vicious, intimate warfare unleashed by secession, climaxing with the destruction of Lawrence, Kansas, by Quantrill's raiders just the year before, 1863, an attempt to raze, to burn out of existence, out of memory that hotbed of Jayhawk abolitionism.

This fratricidal rage expressed itself in raid and counter-raid in the very center of the nation, Missouri, the jumping-off point to the western territories, the state divided between northern and southern sympathies, the state through which ran the very artery of river transportation to the upper Missouri River. No wonder the War of the Rebellion—or the War of Northern Aggression—turned even more vicious and deeply felt than back east. It was like one of those tornadoes that stormed through that country in the spring, a whirling cyclone of pent-up energy gathered and concentrated and furious. Those aren't battles a young man could simply expunge from his soul, forget and set aside. Those are battles that rage in his memory, in his fevered dreams. Those are battles that surge into his words and his deeds on a hot Fourth of July in the nation's innermost port, seemingly far from the battlefields, yet not far at all. The streets of a rough-and-tumble town could become a battlefield too.

A METHODIST MINISTER WITH STRONG SOUTHERN SYMPATHIES crosses the Yellowstone River on the Fourth of July and begins his career as legendary preacher in Montana. Learner B. Stateler, like so many in the new territory, seeks the land of opportunity, but in this case, the opportunity to mine the souls of the outcast, lost miners. He is a man in flight from the fires of disunion, for his house in Kansas had been burned to the ground, his wife and daughter barely escaping. They fled to Denver, only to discover a deep animus toward their regional allegiance, and so they join Jim Bridger's first train along the western flank of the Big Horn Mountains. It will prove an eventful trip, for his wagon tips over a ledge, his wife, horses, and himself rolling twice down the hillside. Fortunately, none is seriously injured, an outcome the good minister attributes to God's grace.

The Statelers will stop briefly in Virginia City, but finding the town overrun and chaotic, he and his wife back track to Norwegian Gulch on the Madison River in the shadow of the Tobacco Root Mountains. Arriving in the emerging diggings on July 20, he sets about building a preaching arbor with sticks and branches, creating a kind of canopy as protection against the blazing sun, and is pleased to see that many miners observe the Sabbath by singing with full voice at his first service in the wilderness.

The Kentucky minister has landed in a just-emerging gold region that will come to be known as the Hot Spring District. At the time of his arrival, two to three hundred miners work the diggings just thirty-five miles north of Virginia City. Since virtually all wagon trains headed for the mining metropolis must pass through this district, many prospectors choose to try their luck here rather than risking all in the fabled Alder Gulch. The appeal would have been obvious to observant emigrants:

> What attracted prospectors to the Hot Spring District was its ample and easily accessed and worked surface values. Geologically, prospectors in the 1860s found in the Hot Spring District quartz vein outcroppings on the surface that held so much free gold it could be separated from the gangue (minerals with no economic worth) by mere pick and shovel.

Rich in spirit but not material goods, Reverend Stateler reports an abundance of rattlesnakes, game, and grass in his new home. He and his wife take up the tasks of grazing their cows, producing milk and butter for sale, and coping with the shockingly high prices for flour, coffee, and other supplies in the new mining region. The minister will preach in the cabins of Willow Creek during the fall of '64, and when the first Protestant church is dedicated in Virginia City on November 6, he will be invited to preach there as well.

LAST CHANCE FOR WHOM AND FOR WHAT?

Every Montana schoolchild learns the story of the "Four Georgians," down on their luck, desperately seeking the find that will ratify all their travels and disappointments and missteps and lost opportunities. A gold strike is like lightning, pulsing the ground with electricity just once in a given spot, and when will that lightning strike happen, and for whom? Of course, like lightning, the eruption of energy can kill, as will happen to William Fairweather, discoverer of Alder Gulch, the richest find of all in the northern tier of the United States, for he will come to nothing but grief with his fondness for liquor.

So when the four seekers (only one of them a Georgian) return to the narrow gulch in what will soon be Helena, they are looking for lightning in a gold pan, confirmation they have uncovered the latest rich and accessible placer lode in this newly created territory. They had wandered far and near in search of that magic, first testing the Kootenai River region, then traveling north into the Marias River country, deep into Blackfeet territory, suggesting the depth of their despair and need. They had held this secret Last Chance Gulch in their back pocket, having found promising but hardly spectacular color in a first pass.

And now, full belief, full commitment, all in with confidence in the master strike, the big find, on this July 14th, 1864. Two members of the party stay behind to protect the claim, while two others return to Alder Gulch for the equipment needed to establish camp and extract the gold. The two men's nonchalance, their insouciance, must have been impressively deceptive, for there will be just a few followers on their return to Last Chance. Men so keyed up with gold fever can detect the faintest vibration of success, can read it in the men's overeager gestures, their brisk walk, their urgent stares and requests for supplies at Dance & Stuart. What's the rush, boys? Which way you headin'? Where are your partners? Why are you packin' so much for a mere chance at wealth? In contrast with the stampede from Bannack to Alder the summer before, a small party of prospectors travels hopefully to the site 120 miles north. Reginald "Bob" Stanley, one of the famous Georgians (though in fact British by birth), will recall,

The stampeders coming in in 1864 were, first, a party of seven or eight; the second, about fifteen....After these other parties continued to arrive daily—many of them only to stay for the night and leave in the early morning. One cause of their disgust was the small water supply....

In time, a veritable army will descend on the obscure gulch, to tear it to bits and leave the mess and fight and die in hurdy-gurdy houses and back streets.

Last chance for whom? Watching it all, no doubt perplexed and furious, the peoples who have lived here for far longer than any town has existed in this region. This open, welcoming valley, rimmed by mountains east, west, north, and south, warm and bright during the winter months, has been a prime location for Bannock, Shoshone, Nez Perce, Salish, and Piegan hunting parties. It is a crucial place, a crossroads, the site of converging trails and paths to buffalo herds, elk and deer, antelope and wolves, chokecherries and berries for pemmican, and chert for arrows and spearheads. The wild-eyed emigrants see none of this. Gold causes the vision to contract, narrow, to see only the color of wealth. The place now called Montana doesn't really exist—only opportunity in a pan, the mind concentrated further by the brutal physical labor of building sluices, shoveling gravel, washing and panning, and doing it all over again, and again, and again.

Last chance for what? The land and the animals and the nations do not really exist, except as a utility or a hindrance. There is the sheer physical challenge of getting the goods to the exploding camp and getting the gold to Benton City for shipping to the States. Of course, being located at the crossroads, ancient and modern, this new fevered camp is perfectly poised to receive and provide, take and give, as freighters move with relative ease along the Mullan Road and south along the Missouri and its tributaries toward towns such as Bannack and Virginia and Nevada. It will be the haulers and the farmers and the ranchers who will benefit most from this geographic coincidence, for they will be the ones to extract a nice living from the weary, broken-backed laborers in the gold camps. Malcolm Clarke's newly established ranch and road house just to the north in the Little Prickly Pear Valley is positioned to take advantage of this opportunity, as will be the towns of Bozeman and Missoula, emerging later in this year of Montana's creation.

The gulch will become known as "Helena," named for a community in Minnesota. Once again names are symbolic, reflecting a tilt toward the North among early arrivals. Yet this Last Chance Gulch will spur discovery of a mining district with a very different orientation and flavor, Confederate Gulch, just thirty-five miles to the southeast and nearly as productive as these latest diggings, discovered by Southern men in December of '64.

Diamond City, Confederate Gulch, Montana, ca. 1870-1871. MONTANA HISTORI-CAL SOCIETY RESEARCH CENTER PHOTOGRAPH ARCHIVES, HELENA, MONTANA

Pretty Shield. MONTANA HISTORICAL SOCIETY RESEARCH CENTER PHOTO-
GRAPH ARCHIVES, HELENA, MONTANA

AUGUST

In which the Crows defend their homeland against the Sioux and Cheyenne, James Fergus sends an angry letter to Pamelia, his wife, Bull Lodge becomes a great leader of the A'aninin, John Bozeman founds a town, and Victor Charlo describes home.

August is the moon that ends the summer holy encampment, the crows begin to gather or bunch up, the moon to move back to their hunting areas to stock up on meat for their winter use.

CROW TRIBAL HISTORY TELLS:

> The outnumbered Apsáalooke successfully defended themselves against the combined forces of the Lakota, Cheyenne and Arapaho on East Pryor Creek north of present-day Pryor, Montana. The largest and most dramatic battle to protect eastern Apsáalooke lands from the Lakota invasion of the 1860s.

Pretty Shield tells:

> Once when the Lacota and Cheyenne came together against us our village was on Arrow [Pryor] creek. They were five to our one. There seemed to be little chance for the Crows, when my father rode through the village on a gray horse. He had stripped, and painted his face and body yellow. Zigzagging through the yellow paint, lengthwise, there were shivery lines that were like those

one sees dancing over hot fires on the plains when the air is clear. These lines made it difficult to see my father, who was singing his medicine-song: "I am the bird among the prairie-dogs."

He gave the Crow war-cry, and then, armed with only his medicine, the stuffed skin of the long-legged owl, tied on his head, and his coup-stick, he rode out alone against the enemy. So strong was his medicine that the Lacota and Cheyenne could not stand against him. They opened, scattered, and then the Crows were upon them, winning a great victory, because of my father's medicine, the long-legged owl that lives with the prairie-dogs.

PLENTY COUPS TELLS:

We swung our lines around our village, riding out from it so that bullets would not reach our lodges. I have never seen a more beautiful sight than our enemy presented. Racing in a wide circle, Sioux, Cheyenne, and Arapahoe gave their war-cries and fired at us from their running horses. But they were not near enough. Their bullets fell short. Iron-bull had ordered us not to fire a shot until the enemy was very close, and then to aim at the middle of the mark, just where a man's body sits on his horse, so that our bullets would kill or cripple either horse or rider. At the shooting by the enemy our line halted. Our village and we ourselves were inside the line of the enemy, who did not come any nearer, but kept circling and wasting bullets. But he made a fine show with his beautiful bonnets and fast horses, some of them our own....

The fight had now left me behind. Our warriors were driving the enemy away, and on both sides of Arrow

Plenty Coups, 1880. National Anthropological Archives, Smithsonian Institution [#3404-A]

Creek the Sioux, Cheyenne, and Arapahoe were being whipped. I forgot to tell you we had help that day. There were forty lodges of Nez Perce visiting us when the enemy attacked, and their warriors helped us, as they should have done under the circumstances. The Nez Perce were not always friendly to us. There was sometimes war between us. But this time they were our friends, and always their warriors are brave men. If it had not been for them we might have been badly whipped ourselves.

As it was we lost a good many men, and so did the enemy. However, we took over two hundred head of their horses and, as soon as we were able moved our village to a better position, expecting another attack. Swan's-head, who was still living, I helped to hold on a horse as we moved. When he breathed I could hear his breath gurgling in the bullet holes....

A historian of the Lakota Sioux tells:

...As daylight spread over the Pryor Creek valley of southern Montana, a great war party of Oglalas and Cheyennes, augmented by Miniconjous and a few Arapahos, approached the main Crow village. Below them the creek swung in a wide curve, and downstream many Lakota women and older men dismounted atop a bluff that afforded a commanding view of the valley. Behind the bluffs, the warriors paused to put on their war gear and prepare their horses.

After stripping to breechclout and moccasins, Crazy Horse rubbed his pony down with sprigs of sage, murmuring words of encouragement. Then, following the instructions of the man from the lake, he took a pinch of dust from a pocket gopher burrow and rubbed it between the war pony's ears. He scattered a handful of the dust over the horse's head, then threw another handful over its rump. After brushing off the excess, he rubbed the dust gently into the horse's skin in streaky lines. He tipped out a little more of the dust and spat into his palm, dabbing one or two spots into his hair....

Along a broad front, individual warriors clashed in daring combat. Young Man Afraid of His Horse, his pony shot twice in the breast, pursued one dismounted Crow almost to the lodges. Elsewhere He Dog overhauled a fleeing Crow, counting coup with the Crow's own saber. But no warrior outshone Crazy Horse. At the head of the charge, he galloped through a hail of arrows and lead, shadowed by young Kicking Bear. A dismounted Crow fleeing for the tipis attracted his attention, and he heeled his pony forward. In the melee, his pony was struck, and Crazy Horse vaulted from the saddle to pursue his foe on foot. Right up against the lodges he caught the Crow, and in a single combat killed him, scalped him, and threw the lifeless body against a tipi. With a whoop of triumph, he withdrew, still unharmed, to join his men. They gathered around him in a protective cluster, crying out his name in tribal pride.

A TIRED MINER IN VIRGINIA CITY COMPOSES A LETTER TO HIS wife, his ire rising as he writes:

Mrs. Fergus I have not had an opportunity to give you my private opinion of the disgraceful scene that took place before Mr. Gilpatrick Thomas Dillin and your own family at dinner one day last week in which you made use of such language as never fails to disgrace or at the very least

lower a female in the estimation of all respectable people.
Profane language is allowable to men by common custom
but when used by a woman it is generally allowed that
she only has to add drinking and then she is prepared to
become a public woman. They are the only women whom
everybody expects to hear swear and even some of them
have never stooped so low.

I have worked hard for my family for some years at very
dirty laborious work have done my own cooking and
washing have gone poorly clad that I might send all my
earnings to my family notwithstanding my old age and
few men of any age have done that or worked so [hard]
as I have. I have had few vegetables have been out most
of the summer on bread and bacon my blood is in bad
order so is that of my family I have kept myself tolerably
healthy by using little salt or as little salted food as possible. I have learned from the best physicians and the best
medical works that salt is not healthy without vegetables
this is the judgement of the civilized world and before my
family came here I lived accordingly I have spoken to you
often on this subject and wrote to you about it before you
left home. On the day in question I told you that a certain
article of food was too salt[y], a good woman would have
felt sorry that such was the case, would say that she would
try to be more careful in the future and would try [to do]
so. In place of that you [chose] to stir up discord or for
some other reason said it was not too salt[y] and that you
could not taste any salt in it.... Such scenes only tend to
degrade us to a level both in my eyes and in that of all
good citizens...and more than that it embitters my life in
my old age.

And so James Fergus rages at his wife, Pamelia, in a private letter. He will never send this letter through the unreliable mail service, since they live together in Virginia City. A contemporary reader wonders why a husband would communicate with his wife in this fashion rather than speaking to her directly. Pamelia and the couple's four children had arrived in the mining town on August 14, after a two-year separation from James. Despite the couple's best hopes, they are struggling to reestablish a companionate marriage with clearly defined roles for husband and wife.

James's anger seems exaggerated, even absurd, hinting at deeper causes of unhappiness. No doubt sheer exhaustion with mining ventures has worn down the body and temper of the man. He had left for Pikes Peak in 1860 to find the capital to underwrite the couple's experiment in frontier living, Little Falls, Minnesota. As a founder of that town, James had lost everything when floods destroyed the dam he had built in his belief that Little Falls would become a frontier metropolis. When Pikes Peak did not pan out, he returned to Minnesota briefly, then headed for the diggings in then-Washington Territory via the same Northern Overland Expedition that brought Nathaniel Langford to the region. James would later observe of members of the caravan,

> I have often thought that Minnesota got rid of more hard cases the trip I came through in than I ever saw together, broken down lumbermen that would pay nothing, broken down merchants, and scalawags of all sorts.

His journey from Fort Benton to Deer Lodge via the Mullan Road likely brought him briefly into contact with the Vails at Sun River Indian Farm. James landed in Bannack, where he supported himself as much by trades such as carpentry as by mining gold. He witnessed the casual violence of a frontier mining camp, describing how Charles Reeves, William Moore, and John

William Mitchell shot up an encampment of Bannock Indians
with no more provocation than too much whiskey and Reeves'
umbrage when an Indian woman took flight after he abused
her. Despite the evident viciousness of the deed, "Strange to
say not a man of them was hung, only banished, on the ground
that it was not murder to kill Indians, and the white men were
killed accidently." Though he espouses relatively liberal views on
race relations, Indian-white violence was very much on James's
mind during his time in Bannack for different reasons: During
the Sioux uprising in Minnesota in the fall of 1862, father and
husband felt isolated, useless in that remote town, desperately
wondering whether he should return to Little Falls to protect his
loved ones. Lonely and deeply worried about the family he left
behind, James carried the responsibilities of supporter, father,
and husband heavily. A steady correspondence between James
and Pamelia told the story of his anxiety, solicitousness, judg-
mental nature, and strong sense of the husband's authority.

But consider Pamelia's challenges as a mining "widow" (her
phrase). She must not only care for her children, but she must
master her husband's troubled business concerns in Little Falls.
She must contend with the terrifying threat of Indian attacks
during the Sioux War. One of her acquaintances captures the
mood of the time in her memorable statement,

> General Pope has been sent up among them to wipe [the
> Sioux] off the face of the earth, but I am afraid it will be
> like the Southern war it will be easier talked of than done.

Pamelia must also serve as chaperone and guide to the couple's oldest daughter, Mary Agnes, who would become engaged
and marry without her father's formal permission. Then, when
James calls Pamelia to join him in Virginia City in early winter
1863, where he seems to have at last struck upon a mother lode
that can support the family, she must complete all preparations
for the family's migration to the remote West. Their journey will

Pamelia and James Fergus. Montana Historical Society Research Center Photograph Archives, Helena, Montana

begin along the Oregon Trail through Nebraska and Wyoming, and then, turning northwest along the trail newly blazed by Jim Bridger, trace a course west of the mighty Big Horn Mountains to the Yellowstone River. The Ferguses will complete their quest by following the road marked out by James Stuart and John Bozeman the previous summer.

Pamelia and her four children, Mary Agnes, Louella, Andrew, and Lillie, along with Mary Agnes's husband, would travel in three covered wagons, each pulled by three teams of oxen. They would need to carry many supplies for the overland trip, as well as many more for setting up house in the mining town, including six hundred pounds of flour, one hundred pounds of rice, four hundred pounds of sugar, a camp stove, frying pans, a large cook stove, a bread pan, water buckets, table dishes, matches, a half-dozen good brooms, feather beds, a suit of clothes for James, four pairs of everyday shoes and two pair of boots for mother and daughters, two reams of good white letter paper, two gold pens for the girls, one box of steel pens and holders, two large bottles of ink, and two dozen lead pencils. Pamelia insists on bringing a sewing machine, complete with an assortment of needles, threads, and yarn, and especially a heavy-duty needle for sewing buckskin. And of course, thinking of his business at hand, James calls for gold pans, a pair of gold scales, a pair of spectacles, some padlocks, two half-boxes of window blaze, two kegs of assorted nails, a few papers of assorted screws, and a package of shoe tacks for miners' boots.

After a month-long, tedious, mud-splattered journey across Iowa, on May 6 the Ferguses arrive in Omaha, jumping-off point for the Platte River Road, only to discover a crowded trail with much of the grass for livestock already under stress. The men James had recruited as drivers and protectors for the family prove a major disappointment, leading Pamelia to write her husband, "…next time I cross the planes it will be with my husband or on my own hook this is the awfless mess I ever was in." Pamelia also travels in deep fear of Indian attack, in part because of the Sioux conflict two years earlier, in part because of the many stories of Indian atrocities heard on the trail. She takes some comfort in seeing many campfires strung along the wagon road at night, signs of aid in case of an emergency. At last, after a four-month trek, Pamelia and the children arrive at their new home in mid-August.

And what is Virginia City like? Visiting Presbyterian minister Jonathan Blanchard observes with evident disgust, "Avarice is everywhere hard, withered and grasping. But it is dreadful here." Yet the new arrivals must have been pleasantly surprised by the amenities available in this frontier town: a bookstore, stationer's shop, bakery, lumberyards, drug emporium, photographic gallery, boot shop, and reading room. The town also offered varied forms of popular entertainment, including a minstrel show, dramatic performances by local actors, prizefights, and lectures.

As James's angry letter reveals, however, coming together as a family after two years of separation would be fraught and painful. No doubt both Pamelia and James had changed in fundamental ways since he first left for the west in 1860. Forced by circumstance to exercise her judgment, Pamelia would not so readily abide by her husband's moods and demands. For his part, James would need to accommodate himself to the needs, desires, and rhythms of his children after years of following his own patterns and whims. The workload for both wife and husband would remain daunting, for despite their best efforts to ease their life by transporting essential supplies from the States, they faced the back-breaking labor of maintaining a house, procuring food and milk, extracting wealth from the mining claims, and fulfilling duties as deputy recorder, president of the Fairweather Mining District, election judge, and county commissioner.

Yet Pamelia and James would live a long life together in Montana, first moving to Last Chance Gulch, then to a ranch outside Helena, then to a spread thirty miles north of Lewistown near the Judith Mountains. But as their testy early days in Virginia City reveal, the transition from separation to union was not always an easy one, and the sheer labor of making a go in an isolated outback of the United States did not assure harmony of purpose and words. The Ferguses stand as a reminder of the human challenge—the toll—of settling in a land distant from a Midwestern home. They also show the costs and benefits of restless male energy let loose on the high plains of the West, for James's insistence on moving time and again to find elbow room required frequent uprootings and replantings. Perhaps it is not surprising that after all these moves, following Pamelia's death in 1887, James will devote his remaining fourteen years to life on the ranch, becoming, in his own words, a kind of hermit. He will regret he can no longer share his life's journey—and his thoughts—with his departed wife.

ON THE 23RD OF AUGUST, GAD UPSON, AGENT TO THE BLACK-feet tribes, distributes annuities promised by treaty to the Gros Ventre nation at Cow Island on the Missouri River. He reports that while the amount of the annuities is less than in the past, the Indians seem to receive the goods with appreciation, though one observer, William Gladstone, describes the scene as pandemonium. Upson counts two hundred and thirty-three lodges, suggesting a total of 1,864 Gros Ventres camped near what they call the Big River. Upson's additional observations are telling. He considers the Gros Ventres the best governed of the tribes he has encountered during his brief time in Montana, and indeed, the best looking and most civilized. More importantly, he reports their head chief, Far-ma-see or Sitting Squaw, is a great friend of the whites, so much so that he offers his tribe's aid to General Sully in his war with the Sioux along the Yellowstone River. Upson concludes, "I do not anticipate any trouble from this tribe; they occupy the extreme eastern portion of the Blackfeet lands, in the vicinity of Milk river, near its mouth. They speak a different language from the other tribes of the nation and appear to be an entirely different race of people."

Perhaps Bull Lodge, a revered medicine man, is among those who receive annuities from Upson. What the Indian agent surely does not know is that in 1819, on Black Butte east of the Judith Mountains, not far from where James and Pamelia Fergus establish their ranch in 1880, Bull Lodge received the first of seven visions that prepared him to become chief medicine man among the A'aninin, the White Clay People.

Bull Lodge's story reveals a people for whom the land of what is now called Montana was sacred, saturated in wonder and spiritual power. His story further reveals that greatness among the White Clay People required determination, discipline, sacrifice, and sustained excellence, for he would not achieve status as chief medicine man until he was sixty-six years old. Bull Lodge's seven visions, and the life he led as a result of those visions, mark a culture, a way of life deeply immersed in the place that Upson would know only superficially, filtered through the lens of his bureaucratic tasks and transparent self-promotion.

Bull Lodge's quest for status as medicine man and warrior began formally at the age of twelve, that liminal moment in the boy's life as he crosses into manhood. This particular youth showed a remarkable dedication, a seriousness of purpose about assuming leadership among his people. He focused his mind on the sacred Feather Pipe and cried out to the Supreme Being for guidance. He received visions of an old man, his face painted like that of the holder of the Feather Pipe, who assured young Bull Lodge that he would become a healer and leader and be lifted out of the poverty that has marked his life as the child of a mixed-blood marriage, his father, Crooked Rump, a French trader whom his Gros Ventre mother had left behind to live with her people. In another vision, Bull Lodge received a magic shield that he is assured will protect him from injury, a shield that will take on added meaning as the seven visions unfold.

This earnest spiritual seeker approached his initiation with due humility, an understanding of his dependence on higher powers and a dedication to the needs of his people.

The seven visions proper commenced in Bull Lodge's seventeenth year. Each revelation took place on one of the high points defining the A'aninins' sacred world: Black Butte, Grows Tallest Butte, Last Butte, Scraper Butte, Bearpaw Butte, Gold Butte, and Porcupine Butte. Americans designated these places by names such as the Sweetgrass Hills and Bears Paw Mountains. The first and most arduous of the vision quests defined the pattern for all seven. Bull Lodge retreated to Black Butte, removed his clothes, and ascended to the top of the landform. Having sacrificed the tip of the little finger on his left hand, he collapsed from loss of blood and a six-day fast. An old man appeared to him in a dream and explained that Bull Lodge had proved his seriousness of purpose and each successive vision would be less daunting. The second quest would require a six-day fast, the third a five-day quest, and so on. The old man assured him that he would become a great medicine man among the A'aninin, but before achieving that status, he must complete the seven ceremonies. The old man further showed him two gifts, a horse and a tipi, and shared that Bull Lodge would receive meaningful aids in each stage that would prepare him as a military leader and healer of the sick. On the eighth day, Bull Lodge, barely able to make his way to the base of Black Butte, was met by his friend Sits Like a Woman, who helped him dress and return to camp.

And so this unfolding series of visions would reveal to Bull Lodge the means to fulfill his destiny. After he offered himself up to the Supreme Being by crying out like a lost child, strips of flesh would be sacrificed and a fast would purify and weaken the seeker. A child would appear to the young man in a dream and lead him to a lodge inhabited by old people, wise elders who shared vital knowledge. In the second vision Bull Lodge would be instructed in the use of the battle shield made manifest to

him as a twelve-year-old; in the third he would gain horses, the
tail feather of a woodpecker, and wealth; in the fourth he would
be instructed in how to use the woodpecker's tail feather to heal
tumors; in the fifth he would receive medicine for five painful
experiences that afflicted the Gros Ventres: consumption, fits,
childbirth, gun wounds, and headaches; in the sixth he would
learn that "people all around you will be your children" and
he would come to know how the white buffalo robe and shield
would provide protection in battle; in the seventh he received
the whistle to heal gunshot wounds.

Despite his piety and dedication, Bull Lodge had not realized
his identity as warrior and medicine man upon completing the
seven visions in his twenty-third year. A'aninin spirituality carried a deeply ethical impulse, such that visions alone did not define the seeker's status as healer and leader. Instead, Bull Lodge
had to enact the revealed wisdom through inspired war deeds
and healing rites. He would serve first as war leader, taking Crow
lives and avoiding injury through the powers of buffalo robe and
shield disclosed to him during his seven visions. (Plenty Coups
would mention Bull Lodge as a respected, feared adversary.)

Then, at the age of forty, a mature man with extensive battle
experience, Bull Lodge renounced the role of war leader and
dedicated himself to healing and curing. He demonstrated the
efficacy of the revealed medicines, tail feather, and whistle by
healing an uncle sick with consumption, a young girl dying of
the fits, and a warrior shot through the chest. At the moment
Upson is distributing annuities to the Gros Ventres at Cow Island on that August day in 1864, Bull Lodge has already become
a widely respected healer for his people at the age of sixty-two.

And yet his spiritual growth is not completed, for within
four years, Bull Lodge will receive the Chief Medicine Pipe, also
called the Feathered Pipe, and so become the chief medicine
man for his people. He will spend the next nineteen years fulfilling his profound responsibilities, including saving wounded

warriors and controlling the weather to aid his people. As the holder of the Feather Pipe, he would "distribute robes (the offerings made by petitioners) used to cover the Pipe to the 'poor and needy old folks.' Keepers entertained anyone who came to pray with a sacred pipe bundle. A prominent man was expected to entertain guests at meals every day, and he provided tobacco to elderly men. His wives invited women from needy families to help prepare the meals in return for part of the food. Men with many horses were expected to lend them to those without." In the end, however, he will not be able to realize the most profound prophecy of all, his resurrection, for the simple reason that the buffalo robes needed to complete the ceremony will no longer be available. The bison will have been exterminated in A'aninin country.

These moving, instructive stories of Bull Lodge remain alive because his daughter, Garter Snake, shared them through her oral storytelling, reminding of the combined power of memory and the spoken word to transmit crucial spiritual and cultural knowledge. This beloved daughter concluded her father's life story with these words:

> Now I have passed through the experience of living over my father's awful death. I feel relieved that I have accomplished what my father, Bull Lodge, expected of me. I have been very careful not to tell you what I didn't know by filling in gaps with my imagination. There are some things I don't know which are missing from this story. You must remember that I am a woman, and that there are parts of his life he did not tell me about for that reason. But now, although I have suffered greatly in the telling of his life story, I am glad that the voice of my father, Bull Lodge, will always be heard. He died in his eighty-fifth year.

AT A MEETING HELD BY THE SETTLERS OF UPPER East
Gallatin at "Jacobs Crossing" on Tuesday, Aug. 9, 1864,
J.M. Bozeman was Elected Chairman and W.W. Alderson
Secretary. The Chairman Stated the object of the meeting to be to form a Claim Association for the purpose
of making laws, etc., in relation to Farming Claims and
for mutual protection. On Motion of W.W. Alderson, it
was Resolved 1st that the Town and District be called
Bozeman.

2nd. That the Boundary of the district shall be as fol-
lows. Commencing at the North East Corner of Kimball's
Claim thence East to the base of the mountains. Thence
in a Southerly direction around the base of the mountains
to Gallatin River thence down said River to a point due
west of said Kimball's claim, thence East to the place of
beginning. Resolved 3rd. That after any Settler Stakes out
and Records a Claim he must be an actual settler within
ten days thereafter in order to hold said claim. On motion
J.M. Bozeman was Elected Recorder, and the sum of One
Dollar the fee for Recording a claim.

And so the town of Bozeman is born just two months after
the creation of Montana Territory. The founders want to get a
jump on the settlers who will no doubt flood into this fertile
valley in order to "mine the miners" by raising crops and cattle
and serving as the trading intermediaries between the laborers
in the mines and the many businesses that would provide them
the equipment and supplies essential for survival in this tough
northern Rockies climate. A traveler passing through on August
18, just nine days after the formation of the claim company, re-
calls that John Bozeman and a partner

spoke eloquently of its many advantages, its water privileges, and its standing right in the gate of the mountains

ready to swallow up all the tenderfeet that would reach the territory from the east, with their golden fleeces to be taken care of.

THE SETTING SEEMS IDEAL, GIVEN THE FERTILE LAND CREATED by the Gallatin River and its many tributaries and the town's location on the main road leading miners west from the Oregon Trail. Of course, this is not the first town so projected and platted in the area—the original effort, Gallatin City, located to the west near the Three Forks of the Missouri, has proved a bust, mainly because of the extensive flooding that ensued for the first settlers in that lush but changeable place.

And who exactly is this John M. Bozeman, who has lent his name to a town, a pass, and a trail? As with many of the first white men to arrive in the gold-rush years, his past is hardly transparent. In truth, he does not seem to have lived an exemplary life, and his future is very much a make-it-up-as-you-go affair. A son of Georgia, and so representative of the many Southerners who have found their way to the new territory, Bozeman had been abandoned by his own father at the age of fourteen, when California gold rush fever carried the paterfamilias to the far West. Bozeman repeated history by following a similar path in 1860 to pursue wealth in Colorado, leaving behind his wife Cathrine and three children, whom he would never see again. As he wrote to his mother in 1866, explaining his absence,

> Tell Cathrine I would like to pay her and the children a visit but I do not know when I can as my Business is in this country and I cannot leave it very well and I am getting pretty well weaned off from the States and any way the Emigration is heavy to this country this season and times are good as could be expected.

John M. Bozeman. Montana Historical Society Research Center
Photograph Archives, Helena, Montana

Contemporary accounts of the man, which tend toward the
sketchy and evasive, suggest he was not one to embrace the hard
work of placer mining. Instead, he is described as a ladies' man,
a gambler, and a masterful promoter, especially of himself. In
this sense John Bozeman is an American type of the first order,
the man on the make in search of opportunity in what will come
to be called the service industries—in his case, the services of
guiding wagon trains along his eponymous trail the summers
of 1863 and 1864 and of conceiving, forming, and promoting
a town that could serve as the trade and agricultural center for
the mining towns to the west and north. The phrase "mine the
miners" is often attributed to Bozeman, though that attribu-
tion may be apocryphal. Whether or not the town's founder can
claim priority in use of the phrase, it perfectly summarizes his
philosophy of making a go in the emerging West.

It would be remiss to ignore the signs of Bozeman's courage
and persistence. A contemporary reader struggles to recapture
the sheer insecurity of life for young American men in the mid-
1800s. They are truly alone and solely dependent on their own
resources. Consider the case of a youth who has been abandoned
by the father who might at least supply a semblance of order and
security. Consider such a youth coming of age in the slave South
with no status through breeding, education, or possession of
slave property. Consider a youth hearing wild tales of adventure
and wealth to be had for the taking—with the only prerequi-
sites being guts and hard work—in the true meritocracy of a
gold boom in a place claimed only by Indians and wild animals,
and shown the way toward that democracy of greed by his own
father. Consider the dilemma posed by the unmistakable signs
of a national drift toward war, toward the divided house coming wholly undone, and the risk that would pose for one's life
and honor. Perhaps such a young man, while loyal to his home
state and region, might have reason to pause at the thought of

sacrificing his life to sustain a way of life that has done little for himself and his family.

Whatever the obscure foreground of Bozeman's presence in Montana, he cuts a dashing figure, over six feet tall with blond-ish hair and blue eyes (how often these founders take on the looks of a Hollywood western, as though the sheer giddiness of getting there first transformed all takers into nearly religious icons of western daring and dash). When leading a wagon train of would-be miners in 1864, he dons the guise of frontier guide, a kind of Natty Bumppo (or is it Jim Bridger?), by wearing a fringed buckskin jacket and slinging a gaudy gunpowder horn over his shoulder. If it is good to be shifty in a new country, it is especially good to be shifty through apt costuming and poses. Still, blazing the trail soon to be named after him in 1863 was no small achievement. Bozeman locked arms with one John Ja-cobs, an occupant of the Deer Lodge Valley who had married a Flathead wife and often guided travelers through the Northwest. With his usual eye for the main chance, Bozeman recognized in Jacobs a kindred spirit, and one with far more knowledge of lo-cal geography than himself. They formed a partnership based on the premise that a faster route to the new mines existed than that offered by following the Emigrant Trial all the way to Corinne, Utah, then turning north to travel through sere high plateau country.

And so, in spring 1863, Bozeman, Jacobs, and eight-year-old daughter Emma Jacobs leave Bannack City to pursue a trail very similar to that taken by James Stuart's Yellowstone Expedition. Like Stuart, they follow the path of William Clark on his return journey to the States in 1806. They have a simple, intuitive plan: In a land shaped by rivers, it should be possible to trace a line from the Oregon Trail to the Idaho mines by following the val-leys of the Powder, Big Horn, Yellowstone, and Madison rivers. Voyagers would simply need to cross one major pass, the divide between the Yellowstone and Missouri river basins (hence its early name, Yellowstone Pass). Bozeman and Jacobs follow this precise path in reverse, giving the former a chance to visit his 160-acre claim in Gallatin City, the failed first township in the lush valley.

But theirs is a tense, dangerous journey, one that surely should have given fair warning of the troubles that would plague the Bozeman Trail during its brief existence (1864 to 1866). Though reputed to be accommodating to whites, Crows intercept them twice on their trek, finally stripping them of everything they have along the Big Horn River. James Stuart glimpses Bozeman shortly before this dire encounter with hostiles, but the small party is eager to flee from contact with anyone of a suspicious cast in the still-unknown Big Horn River valley. The Indians are incensed by the presence of Emma, a mixed-blood child, beating her with a ramrod for fraternizing with these explorers casting about in their beloved, protected country. Sadly, such beatings are familiar to the young girl, since her father indulged in them often for reasons far less clear. Bozeman and Jacobs aren't fooling anyone—they give away the game through their gear and gestures, showing every sign they are blazing a path for many more whites to invade the homeland.

Of course, Bozeman being Bozeman, he doesn't take the hint. Instead, he and Jacobs organize a small party of forty-six wagons and eighty-nine men, as well as some women and children, to put the new trail to the test in July of '63. There is money to be made, a gamble to be had by trail blazers and emigrants alike. Would you put yourself in the hands of this seeming Southern gentleman if it meant cutting six weeks off the dangerous journey to the Idaho mines? Questions abound: Would there be sufficient grass for the many oxen, cattle, and horses you bring with you in this quest for a new life? Would the water be alkaline or potable for people and animals? Would there be sufficient game to feed one and all? And most importantly, would the Indians allow safe passage? Even the most untutored voyager would have heard tales of atrocities and have a sense that Bozeman's path takes them through the homelands not just of the Crows but also of the fearsome Sioux, Cheyenne, and Arapaho.

This first wagon train to follow the Powder River trail makes it as far as Lodge Pole Creek in what will become northern Wyoming before encountering a large gathering of Cheyenne and Sioux men, women, and children. The native peoples inform the train's leaders that if they turn back to the Oregon Trail, there will be no repercussions, but if they continue, the amassed warriors will be compelled to attack the party. As one member of the train later reported the Indians' warning,

> That was the only extensive game country remaining in the West; the California and Oregon Trails had driven most of the antelope and buffalo away from the wagon roads and the result would be the same here; the Indians were determined to prevent the opening of this new road, as it would mean starvation to their squaws and papooses; if we wished to return to the Platte, well and good; if not, all the Sioux and Cheyennes, already warned by nightly signal fires on the Big Horn mountains, would collect and wear us out.

Members of the train had a surprisingly difficult time deciding whether to accede to the Indians' demands, yet, in the end, they seem to take the wise course by reluctantly turning back.

Bozeman, however, will not take no for an answer, since he leads a party of nine men on a kind of midnight ride through this wild country all the way to Bannack, in part to expedite his return to home base in order to plan for the coming year of leading trains, in part to demonstrate his bravado and toughness. One participant in this cross-country sprint writes of the company's leader,

> Mr. Bozeman's restless activity and love of adventure prevented his possible contentment in any mining camp.… He was genial, kindly and as innocent as a child in the ways of the world. He had no conception of fear, and no matter how sudden a call was made on him day or night, he would come up with a rifle in his hand. He never knew what fatigue was, and was a good judge of all distances and when you saw his rifle level you knew that you were not to go supperless to bed.

It is tempting to be skeptical of this claim for Bozeman's innocence, since he seems to have calculated wisely and well how to insinuate himself into many schemes (a popular word at the time) yielding monetary rewards, and he further seems to ignore Indian nations' rightful claims to protection of their homelands guaranteed by treaty. But at this great distance in time, perhaps it is unfair to accuse the pioneer of disingenuous behavior—better to trust the perspicacity of the contemporary observer. Certainly Bozeman's mysterious death will raise questions about his insight into the motives of others.

Following his exploits on the Powder River trail, the still-young Georgian forms a company with like-minded entrepreneurs in Virginia City, gaudily titled the Missouri and Rocky Mountain Wagon Road and Telegraph Company. This rather comprehensive name captures the audacious reach of these businessmen, focused on consolidating control of Bozeman's cutoff to the mines by creating a series of toll gates and toll ferries along the route. The list of fellow founders reads like a roll call of prominent pioneers: Samuel Hauser, Nathaniel Langford, Samuel Word, and W.B. Dance (who had entered into the mercantile business with the Stuarts). To effect this grand plan, Bozeman heads south to Salt Lake City in late '63, then east to gather emigrants for the 1864 wagon train season. Jim Bridger is part of the scheme as well, for he accompanies Bozeman on this sojourn to Laramie to wrangle the tenderfeet. Apparently the company founders had the foresight to anticipate that Bozeman's proposed path, blocked the previous summer by determined Indians, might have to give way to Bridger's preferred route along the west side of the Big Horns, thereby avoiding the prime hunting grounds offered by the Powder River. But as John Owen's journal revealed, experience would prove Bridger's route untenable.

On that August day of Bozeman City's creation, then, the town's namesake has recently arrived in the Gallatin Valley via the route he had been forced to abandon in '63, demonstrating to his satisfaction the cut-off's viability. It had been a relatively easy journey, but he was by no means alone in testing the tolerance of the Sioux and Cheyenne for these interlopers. In fact, four trains comprised of approximately 1,500 emigrants would follow this path in 1864, though one, led by A.A. Townsend, ran into serious difficulty with a Cheyenne war party and lost four men as a result.

John Bozeman is a busy man the fall of 1864 as he seeks to develop and protect his new town. First he recruits Thomas Cover (a figure of some importance later in his life) and P.W. McAdow to build a flour mill near the nascent town, a sure sign of economic stability for prospective farmers. He does everything he can to assure success by capitalizing their mill and introducing them to inhabitants of the valley. Later that fall, roused by an Indian scare in the Gallatin Valley, he places an advertisement to this effect in the Territory's first and only newspaper, the *Montana Post*:

> Captain Bozeman being authorized to raise a Cavalry Company, will attend in person at the Virginia Hotel in Virginia City, from the 20th to the 22d, inclusive of the present month, for the purpose of taking recruits to accompany him in a single expedition in pursuit of maraud-

ing Indians, who have been murdering, robbing and stealing horses. Said expedition will probably last from three
to five weeks. All prizes taken will be equally divided with
the company.

As was his wont, Bozeman fancies himself a "Captain," though
he has no official claim to such a title. The question of whether
Indian depredations in the region warranted raising a force remains open to this day, but Governor Sidney Edgerton denied
authorizing such an expedition. The closing sentence is fascinating for suggesting such a troop would have every incentive
to steal as much as possible from Indians encountered during
those weeks of service. In any case, Bozeman never organizes or
deploys this cavalry company, and so the notice must be ranked
with the many false panics about Indian violence during Montana Territory's early years.

For all his energy, derring-do, and schemes, Bozeman never
amassed significant wealth. Upon his death, his will revealed a
total estate of $1,700, including his property in Bozeman City.
He explained to his mother in a letter home, "I have made a
great amount of money in this country but have had some bad
luck and spent a good deal." Perhaps W.J. Davies, who knew
Bozeman well, comes closer to the truth when he observes in
a reminiscence of the man, "Bozeman had no use for money
except to bet with, and the most congenial place to him on earth
was the saloon, with a few boon companions at a table, playing
a game of draw."

The Georgian lost his life under mysterious circumstances
in 1867, but whatever the exact cause of his death, the incident
suggests a degree of the innocence attributed to him by James
Kirkpatrick. Bozeman and Tom Cover, the very man he had
supported in building a mill the fall of '64, planned a journey to
Fort C.F. Smith on the Big Horn River to obtain flour orders to
support that very mill. The travelers may have also been scout-

ing locations to establish ferries and build a bridge—for tolls, no doubt—on the Yellowstone River. Something went terribly wrong. Bozeman was murdered by a single gunshot wound to his right breast. As the only available witness to the event, Tom Cover's story has held problematic priority in piecing together what happened. By his account, Bozeman made the mistake of trusting five Blackfeet Indians who stopped at their camp to share a meal, and, taken unawares, was gunned down by a devious Indian. However, there were enough inconsistencies and incredible elements to Cover's story to raise the possibility that he himself was the murderer. There was also the little matter of Bozeman's rumored attentions to Cover's wife. Apparently Bozeman trusted someone too much—by Cover's account, those Indian visitors; by others' accounts, Cover himself. The truth will never be known. What can be known is that a tall Georgian abandoned home and family at the age of twenty-five, took a series of risks in the mining regions of the West, showed a remarkable capacity for planning, executing, and marketing an array of money-making plans, and left his name imprinted on a community, a pass, and a trail. Given his modest beginnings, it was quite a life.

FROG CREEK CIRCLE

for my family, especially Jan

Mountains so close we are relative.
Creek so cold it brings winter rain.

We return to warm August home,
Frog Creek, where I've lived so long
that smells are stored, opened only
here. This land never changes, always
whole, always the way we want it to be.
We always come back
to check our senses or to remember
dreams. We are remembered today in circles
of family, of red pine, of old time chiefs,
of forgotten horses that thunder dark stars.

These are songs that we come to this day,
soft as Indian mint, strange as this sky.

Victor Charlo

SEPTEMBER

In which Coth-co-co-na tells the story of her marriage to Malcolm
Clarke, Gad Upson distributes annuities to the allied Blackfeet nations, and James Welch provides an overview of settlement.

September is the moon when the long time rain comes, the de-
parting of the thunder for that year, the yellowing of the leaves,
the gathering of the white fish or sharpface fish, the moon
that dries the berries up. The moon to move to their wintering
areas. To bless all holy bundles and put away for winter.

MALCOLM CLARKE STILL CARRIES THE TOBACCO SACK
she made for him all those years ago, scarlet cloth
with blue beading. He handles it lovingly, often.
Coth-co-co-na surprises herself by focusing on that object of
affection, her gift, when Malcolm returns from this new mining camp just twenty-five miles south of their ranch. She prefers
calling him by his American name rather than the Piegan name,
Ne-so-kei-o, Four Bears, which carries more than a hint of derision. Her people gave him that moniker upon hearing his boast
of slaughtering four grizzlies in a single day. Names are often
a way of humbling as well as honoring men, but her husband
only detects the honor, bragging often about the title and the
exploit to the white men who travel the road through their new
home, the road stretching from Benton City to the new mines
and continuing down to those older mines near the headwa-

ters of the Missouri. No, she prefers "Malcolm." Or else his first Piegan name, White Lodge Pole, a true honorific, signifying his straightness, tallness, and stature.

Malcolm has changed much over the twenty years of their life together. She knows what a hard place this high plains country can be. She knows that the Piegan and the other Indian peoples often require an American trader to be strong, threatening, even violent at times. Force is what they respect, an ability and willingness to meet a challenge with power and guile. Malcolm has accomplished that time and again, and he has made a good life for her and her children. Yet all that striving and fighting have made him a harder man, less able to see the way his actions breed resentment as well as respect. Because he has been fortunate, he does not see the fragility of all he has built.

He loves telling the story of the time he struck a Piegan warrior in the camp of The Calf Shirt, how the band angrily surrounded him, determined to punish him for this violation of their hospitality, how The Calf Shirt spoke then, declaiming his hatred for whites but respect for Malcolm. Yes, he loves telling that story, yet he does not perceive the luck, the good fortune of his salvation. It could so easily have gone the other way, ending with his murder and scalping. She wishes he would stop telling that story.

But Malcolm does not consult her as he once did. While she remains his sitting-beside-wife, Coth-co-co-na has been replaced in his ardor by Akseniski, Good Singing, a much younger mixed blood who has borne him two children. Just this summer she gave birth to a dear girl, Judith, named after the beautiful river valley where she, Coth-co-co-na, bore him children in the early days of their marriage, the place that was, until now, her favorite home. She loves this baby girl like one of her own, but still it hurts that he does not turn to her more often to seek her counsel, especially about his dealings with her kin. Her "cousin" Pete Owl Child remains a troubled young man, uncertain of his

Malcolm Clarke. Montana Historical Society Research Center Photograph Archives, Helena, Montana

place in either the Piegan or American worlds, restless and easily
called to violence. She now believes taking the boy to Ann Arbor
with them was a mistake—it only confused her relative about
the shape and purpose of his life. She too was overwhelmed by
that foreign place, the loud trains and brick buildings and inces-
sant chatter and stark differences in wealth. Part of her admired
the Napikwan like never before, reminded again and again of
their cleverness, their ability to make massive buildings and organize all these frenzied people. Certainly she understood why
her husband wanted her two oldest children, Nellie and Horace,
to spend time there, to learn the ways of the invaders. Malcolm
and Coth-co-co-na talked often of the changes coming to their
world, how the Napikwan would overrun the upper Missouri,
how greed would attract many of the worst whites, how desire
for power would lead them to put the Piegan in a smaller and
smaller box. Malcolm grew red in the face speaking of these
changes, telling his first wife how the Americans desire a great
nation, and how that desire would lead them to bring soldiers
to the northern plains, after the great war in the east ended. She
heard him tell Horace many times, "Side with your mother's
people if it comes to a battle between the Piegan and the Americans." Her heart rings with love for him in moments like that.

But the world is changing, and so her strong, intelligent older
children must learn the ways of the coming people. How Coth-
co-co-na wept the first time she saw her first-born sitting so
forlornly on a mackinaw boat at Fort Benton, about to depart
for St. Louis and a white education. She sobbed so hard she collapsed on the dock, and maybe she was weeping for her people's
way of living, not just for her fragile children, in that big river,
about to journey to a place she had not yet been. How homesick
she grew in Ann Arbor, then, when Malcolm decided to try living in that world rather than facing the prospect of seeing his
fur trade life eroded and erased. But he grew homesick too, and
in part it had to do with Owl Child, a gifted youth, to be sure,

but troubled, something askew in his mind. Even at an early age he showed all the insecurity of a young man from the powerful, militant band of Mountain Chief, never sure of belonging, never sure of respect. Her people placed such a high premium on a man's honor, and Pete always seemed to be reaching for acknowledgment, simple confidence. He boasted too much, rode too hard, hurt people when they only wanted to tease and play. No, Coth-co-co-na now doubted that taking him all that way to that Napikwan town had been a good idea.

She thinks much of her troubled cousin because her Piegan kin have begun to spend time at the new ranch in the Little Prickly Pear Valley. Malcolm has built a trading post on this vital road between Benton City and the new mines, which Malcolm calls "Last Chance Gulch." He couldn't have chosen a more fitting setting, for the Missouri River Valley narrows here, allowing her husband to charge a toll for people as they pass through. He sells whiskey as well, something that goes down well for travelers weary of the dust and heat and fear of travel in a land still dominated by honor-seeking young men from the many nations. And what a storyteller Malcolm has become lately, entertaining his white guests with tales of his fur-trading life, even touching on the death of Owen Mackenzie that caused them to leave behind the trading life altogether. She wishes her husband would not make light of that incident, witnessed by her son Horace, just a year earlier near the junction of the Judith and Missouri rivers. Malcolm insists Mackenzie was just another hard-drinking frontiersman, deserving of this end, but Coth-co-co-na knows that envy of Mackenzie ate at her husband's heart, envy of Mackenzie's relative youth, skill with rifle and horse, and general affection among the whites and natives strung along the Missouri. If she could alter one thing in Malcolm's character, it would be that same quest for honor, for respect that infects Pete and so many of her own people.

As she watches the awe and affection of these powerful white men traveling the Mullan Road, mesmerized by her charming husband, she feels a deep dread in her heart, for herself and for her children. What role will they have in this changing place, this transformed world? She finds herself going back in time often to her early marriage, how proud she was to marry this strong white man, in the simple ceremony at Fort Mackenzie, near the mouth of the Marias River, just twenty years ago, White Lodge Pole giving her father nine horses for her. She could not help being swept up by her husband's energy and courage, his willingness to live in her people's winter camp, not only to show them how to trap the winter animals for trade with his employer, the American Fur Company, but also to show that he knew and cared for them. It was the necessary sign of respect for the very people who would make or break his life as a trader, his willingness to share their often spare meals of pemmican and berries, to wear the clumsy animal skins for protection against the snow and cold, to tolerate the increasing unpleasantness of the winter camp as January turned into February turned into March. His command of the Piegan tongue helped as well, for he could tease with the best of her relatives, give as well as a take, a critical verbal skill in this contest for status. And yes, she could not help shuddering with pleasure at the thought of their early carnal life, how passion swept them up and they could rise to it without check or hesitation.

How Coth-co-co-na would love to hear him tell stories of his life before he came to Piegan country, his time at a military academy, then in this far-off place called Texas, where he helped win independence for that new country, and the lessons he learned there about how a new country attracts the very dregs of his nation, the drammers and the killers who seek a free field for their vices. He would warn her that such men would come to her country in time, he didn't know when they would be called here, but already they were aware of the great road to the west, to Oregon, and a trail through the Piegan country could be a more direct route to that seemingly far-off place near the great water. That was the very meaning of Isaac Stevens' surveying and treaty-making, especially Lame Bull's Treaty in 1855 with the Blackfeet and Gros Ventre nations. Stevens was looking to draw that straight American line through the heart of Piegan country, a vector, an arrow of national will. The Mullan Road is just the forerunner to some future railroad.

Malcolm also told her of the big farms he had seen back east, how the Americans like to raise white horns for meat, and hay to feed them, and wheat to make bread. As he looked around the Missouri and Marias country, he could see how his countrymen would find opportunity here. Above all he tried to make her understand that men in his nation find status and honor in a very different way than the Piegan. If horse-taking, battle coups, and gift giving were the keys to respect for her people, land and property signified status for his people. And given the sheer number of people back east, the desire for land would only expand, leading Americans to claim more and more territory for property. He now believed the Piegan had created a better life for a place like their homeland, better than the settled agricultural life of his people, but that would not stop the Americans from wanting the land. That's one reason he enjoyed occupying the Sun River Indian Farm for a brief time, turning it into his private trade center, renouncing the claim that it could serve as model of a settled life for the Blackfeet tribes.

How she misses those times of sharing, of teaching each other the ways of their very different nations. And now Malcolm has done exactly as he said his countrymen would do, he has claimed Piegan land as property and built this house, barn, and store. He saw the way things were turning, how the gold miners were the advance guard of a settled American way of inhabiting the valleys and plains, and he could raise the wheat and the cattle to feed these new people, assure his full family, two wives and many children, a good life, even after he has passed on. But she knows all that storytelling, all that returning to his youth through words, is a sign of deep restlessness, for he misses the spontaneity, risk, and sheer exuberance of the wide-open fur trading days.

She also knows that her people have changed with the trading in guns, whiskey, tobacco, metal knives, and kettles. Her people chose the trade, desired the goods, and they have lost some of their independence, their wisdom as a result. In truth, they have been taking too many buffalo for exchange, and the great herd seems to be diminishing. She tries to quell a rising uneasiness as she contemplates how her people, especially the young men, have been altered by the goods and the increasing number of invaders. They drink too much of that awful water, they like using the rifles so much that they harm not just whites but also other Piegan, they crave the sugar and coffee and wool coats and hard shoes and firm hats. Her people seem confused, disoriented, in a maze. And again her mind turns to Pete Owl Child, who represents this emerging sickness in her people, deeper and far more dangerous than even the horrific white scabs disease. When Owl Child visited their ranch this summer, with his beautiful wife and many of their relatives, she could feel his envy of Malcolm, his sense of being dishonored by another man's wealth, another man's abundance. She had spent time with that beautiful wife and found her a frivolous creature, intent on spurring her weak husband to strength through ridicule and open mockery. She also senses her husband's attraction to this frivolous woman, and knowing the ways of Malcolm's passion, she fears that might lead where no one should go.

But more than anything, Coth-co-co-na fears for her children, especially her strong, willful older daughter, Nellie. She is truly her father's daughter, tall, straight, but of mixed blood. She has her father's pride, too, shown in her unbending judgment of people less virtuous or intelligent than she. Trained by the Catholic nuns in their strict dogma, eloquent and theatrical, Nellie may well carry the burden of her blended heritage, the Piegan and the American. Coth-co-co-na often thinks her daughter more a chief, more like her own father than is the resourceful but hot-tempered son Horace. Her eldest child will never serve a husband as she has served Malcolm, and so she may face a lonely road. Will those sharp-eyed, greedy Americans she meets so often these days acknowledge her daughter's right to lead? It seems incredible, impossible. In any case, Nellie will become the hostess of the ranch when she returns next summer, her education in that distant town of St. Paul complete and visible. It will take that strong presence to sooth her husband and reassure guests that they are in the company of a civilized family.

Coth-co-co-na will remain in the background, serving rather than calling attention to herself. She will do her best to accommodate this new order, embrace all members of her husband's family, and fend off fears for the future. She will gladly ride one of her husband's splendid horses through this beautiful valley and catch the wind in her graying hair, gripping the reins loosely, letting the roan run free. In that moment she will live again her childhood on the Marias River, daughter of a chief, member of Mountain Chief's band, a proud people unbowed, sure that their world is inviolate, enduring.

GAD UPSON DISTRIBUTES ANNUITIES TO THE ALLIED BLACKfeet tribes at Fort Benton in late September. He counts 400 Piegan lodges, with an estimated population of 2,800. He singles out their leader, Little Dog, for special praise, describing him as the only chief of spirit and action and a great friend of the whites. The Bloods number 1,800 members, but Upson questions the suitability of the treaty arrangement since this nation spends most of the year above the Medicine Line. The agent reserves special censure for the Blackfeet, numbering 100 lodges or approximately 700 members. He objects to their insolence upon confronting the paltry annuities and offers this observation for the benefit of his superiors in Washington:

> I look upon this tribe as being one of the worst in or near this agency, and were it not that the treaty expires next year, would recommend that their next annuity be paid them in powder and ball from the mouth of a six-pounder....

In fairness to Upson, he has expressed frustration over the shortage of annuities, urging the Superintendent of Indian Affairs to investigate graft and corruption in the handling of these promised supplies.

The Blackfeet agent concludes his report with this confident note:

> The general condition of the Indians in this agency is as favorable as could be expected from such wild and savage beings. The great number of whites, together with the expedition of General Sully, that have shown themselves in this country, has had a beneficial influence upon them, and some have foresight enough to perceive that their power over the whites is fast passing away to return no more forever.

THE MAN FROM WASHINGTON

The end came easy for most of us.

Packed away in our crude beginnings
in some far corner of a flat world,
we didn't expect much more
than firewood and buffalo robes
to keep us warm. The man came down,
a slouching dwarf with rainwater eyes,
and spoke to us. He promised
that life would go on as usual,
that treaties would be signed, and everyone—
man, woman and child—would be inoculated
against a world in which we had no part,
a world of money, promise and disease.

James Welch

OCTOBER

In which prospectors stampede Silver Bow Creek, the Chinese settle in German Gulch, the Republicans hold a rally in Virginia City, and Sisters of Providence establish a boarding school at St. Ignatius.

October is the Geese Go South Moon. Certain animals such as the plains rabbit and the weasel begin to turn white for their winter coat.

THE RICHEST HILL ON EARTH BEGINS AS A MODEST GOLD rush in the autumn of 1864. Silver Bow Creek is named poetically by one of the first discoverers of placer deposits in this tributary of the Hell Gate (now Clarks Fork) River, who was taken with the many "silver bows" in the curving, turning, downhill-running stream. William Allison, Pete McMahon, and Bud Parker explore this region in part because of the obvious mineral deposits displayed in the large "butte" that slopes southward toward the creek. They could have no idea of the depth and extent of wealth ensconced in that formation a mile above sea level.

Once they hit pay dirt, the usual rush of prospectors flows north from Alder Gulch, just seventy miles to the south. The center of mining gravity lands about seven miles west of the present town of Butte, though it is no bargain for living: 150 men surviving in temporary tents and lean-tos, braving the winds and heat and snows of a high plateau in the Rockies. When the gold plays out on the Silver Bow, all that grasping energy will turn to silver, which in turn will lead to the greatest find of all, copper. This is the discovery that will make William Andrews Clark extravagantly wealthy.

Perhaps more typical of Butte's early mining days is Frank Beck, who arrives at Silver Bow Creek in December of '64. He is another young American in flight from conflagration, the War Between the States, a teacher and lawyer-in-training who chose the dare of the west over the risk of the battle. He and his brother work claims south of Silver Bow Creek, but Frank soon takes his hard work to the Red Mountain City gold mines south of Deer Lodge, a shrewd move that will build the foundation for an affluent life.

Frank will bring his earnings back to Butte, clearly the rising city, and assume prominent roles as deputy sheriff, marshal, and deputy county treasurer. Like many clever early arrivals in Montana, he seems to have used these various positions to gain precise insight into the financial and personal lives of local inhabitants, giving him an edge in anticipating bargains for the taking and deals for the making. Not surprisingly, then, he will focus on real estate and banking as his means to wealth, and he will succeed to such a degree that an august building, one among many in Butte's historic district, still features his name: J.F. Beck, short for Josiah Francis Beck. At his death he will leave an estate of $80,000, though he will choose to will most of it to charity, leading his widow, Agnes, to contest the will.

Gold prospecting in the Butte area will not be limited to Silver Bow Creek, for miners would find their way to another rich lode:

> In 1864, four German gold prospectors left Bannack, Montana and headed north hoping to find a new big strike around modern-day Butte. After several days of panning for gold in Silver Bow Creek, they went up a

small stream and discovered rich gold sands in what would become German Gulch, named after the first discoverers. Within days of filing a claim on their discovery the area boomed, with hundreds of gold seekers heading into the area. Within a few weeks there were large settlements established at the head and middle of German Gulch, named Upper and Lower Town, respectively. These communities boasted all the amenities of most mining towns of the 1860s including saloons, butcher shops, hotels, restaurants, and even the large Kessler Brewery.

By the late 1860s, most miners of Euro-American descent will sell their claims to Chinese immigrants, revealing the importance of this national group in the rich ethnic mix of early Montana. In fact, the Chinese, working in large groups to share both the risk and the rewards of mining, will produce roughly half of the $1,000,000 in gold extracted from German Gulch. They will also leave behind a rich trove of artifacts, physical evidence of a presence long suppressed in the collective memory of the state:

> Chinese immigrants first came to Montana after the gold discovery at Bannack in 1862. By 1870, the Chinese population exploded, accounting for 10% of the territory's total population, and even higher proportions in urban areas such as Virginia City and Helena....Far from modern centers of population, Chinese dominated the mining communities in Cedar and Gold Creeks, and German and Cave Gulch throughout the late 1860s and 1870s.... German Gulch best reflects the archaeological and historical conditions of the Chinese during the 19th century, with the creation of a nearly self-contained society with its own store, recreational pursuits, and well-paying gold claim. The archaeological recovery of imported Chinese

goods, from coconuts to porcelain serving bowls, illustrates the extensive trade networks existing in Montana before the first railroad even entered the Territory. In apparent affront to the Montana Alien Law, the Chinese owned most of the placer claims in German Gulch during the 1870s and made a substantial profit.

ON SATURDAY, OCTOBER 15, REPUBLICANS GATHER FOR A political rally in Virginia City, determined to elect true believers to Montana's first legislature. As summarized in the *Montana Post*,

> A large and enthusiastic Union ratification meeting was held on Saturday evening last, in Virginia City, Judge Bissell presided. We are happy to say it provided a great contrast to the other—that is, the Grand-Union-Peace-War-North and South Amalgamation Society, humorously called Democrats.

Hezekiah Hosmer, the newly appointed chief justice of Montana Territory, Wilbur Sanders, and Thomas Dimsdale take their turns declaring their loyalty to the Union cause and their disdain for the opposition party. Sanders' words as paraphrased in the article are especially telling: "He had been called an extreme man. He would stand by the Union in every extremity, and he believed in one flag and one destiny for the American nation, but on the slavery question he wished to be understood. Did me think that they degraded themselves by following the footsteps of the missionary, and in the enlightened spirit of true religion, endeavoring to elevate the condition and educate the minds of the fallen—the outcast?"

The rally echoes the invective-laced, hot-blooded, often defamatory political meetings throughout the States as the 1864 presidential election approaches in just three weeks. Lincoln's strong-armed defense of the national union, including suspen-

Wilbur F. Sanders. Photograph by R.A. Lewis, New York City, NY. Montana Historical Society Research Center Photograph Archives, Helena, Montana

sion of habeas corpus, issuance of the Emancipation Proclamation, and the sheer carnage of the United States' most lethal war, has put his reelection in doubt. His main challenger? None other than the castoff general George McClellan, carrying the peace cause on his handsome shoulders. The uncertainty of Lincoln's fate, the very man who has signed Montana into creation and appointed Edgerton governor, gives the Virginia City rally an edge, an intensity that might otherwise be missing.

National Republicans have combined with Democrats supportive of the war to form a National Union Party, a temporary joining of uneasy allies that will sweep the president to a resounding electoral-college victory. Montana's staunch Republican leaders will deploy the same tactic but with little of the success achieved by the commander in chief. The October rally is more given over to destroying enemies than uplifting friends, though attendees very much hope Sanders will be elected the territory's first representative to Congress. There is much talk of disloyalty and failure by opponents to acknowledge the war was forced upon the federal government by seceshes. The result? Sanders goes down to resounding defeat, and Montana's first legislature is evenly divided between Democrats and Republicans, assuring a messy session of creating the territory's founding laws in December.

ON OCTOBER 17, FOUR SISTERS OF PROVIDENCE ARRIVE IN ST. Ignatius, a mission founded in 1854 that now features a church, saw- and grist mills, a cabin for the Jesuit priests, and soon, a cabin for these newcomers. The sisters may be the first white women to cross into Montana Territory from west of the Rockies. Their purpose: To open a girls' boarding school and hospital. A day school commences in December, with tuition of twenty-five dollars a month. It becomes a boarding school in 1865. The Jesuits will also establish a boarding school for boys.

This small historical nugget carries a world of meaning. Indian boarding schools will prove one of the central traumas in Montana's history. Children will be forced to give up their hair and clothing, their languages, and their connection to the land and the people in order to become fully American. Angry teachers will attempt to beat the Indian out of them so that they can live as one culture's definition of a complete human being. Ideas of savagery and civilization undergird this exercise in behavioral and psychological modification. These memories will come down to the present time as a dark symbol of one culture's desire to eradicate many peoples' ways of living, of being.

Antedating the arrival of the Sisters of Providence is the twenty-year history of Catholic presence in the region, beginning in 1841 with the advent of the peripatetic Father Pierre-Jean De Smet. The Jesuit missionary arrived with high hopes: "...the nation of the Flatheads appear to be a chosen people—'the elect of God';...it would be easy to make this tribe a model for other tribes." The mission at St. Mary's in the Bitterroot Valley will flourish for almost a decade, until the Jesuits seek to convert the Blackfeet to their faith, a move the Salish interpret as a betrayal. So it is that John Owen becomes master of this prime location in 1850. The Jesuits' decision to favor their religion over an exclusive relationship with the welcoming Salish suggests that another kind of nationhood, the Catholic faith, takes priority over an alliance with loyal peoples.

But it would be a mistake to believe that De Smet did not sympathize with the native people he came to know so well. He will presciently conclude, of the gold rush to the headwaters of the Missouri,

> One cannot help being anxious for the fate of the Indians on account of the approach of the whites. The treasures concealed in the heart of the mountains will attract thousands of miners from every land; and with them will

come the dregs of civilization, gamblers, drunkards, robbers and assassins.

In part because of this kind of insight, in part because of his indefatigable constitution, in part because of his friendship with a wide range of key players on the upper Missouri, including Alexander Culbertson and Jim Bridger, Father De Smet remained a fixture, a necessity, in the region until the mid-1860s. He was a central player at the treaty gathering near Fort Laramie in '51. He left behind this remarkable description of the place that became Montana as he and Culbertson journeyed with tribal leaders from the Hidatsa, Arikara, and Mandan nations to the Laramie gathering:

> I was for seven days among innumerable herds of buffalo. Every moment I perceived bands of majestic elk leaping through this animated solitude, while clouds of antelopes took flight before us with the swiftness of arrows. The ashata or bighorn alone seemed not to be disturbed by our presence.... Deer are abundant, especially the black-tailed deer....All the rivers and streams that we crossed in our course, gave evident signs that the industrious beaver, the otter and the muskrat were still in peacable possession of their solitary waters. There was no lack of ducks, geese, and swans.

It is a world that would not last, at least not in this variety and fecundity.

De Smet is also asked to intercede with the Sioux the summer of 1864 to encourage them to put aside combat and negotiate peace before Alfred Sully's troops march into their heartland. His mission proves futile, a failure he will lay at the feet of Sully, who avers he has been ordered to punish all Indians who have killed white men. In De Smet's words,

Father Pierre-Jean de Smet, ca. 1860-1865. LIBRARY OF CONGRESS

> In consequence of the General's declaration and the cir-
> cumstances of the case, my errand of peace, though sanc-
> tioned by the Government, became bootless and could
> only serve to place me in a false position—that of being
> face to face with the Indians without being able to do
> them the least service. So I took the resolution of return-
> ing to St. Louis.

De Smet will take this disappointment to Washington City
this very year and share his disgust with the Superintendent of
Indian Affairs, using the occasion to sue for more Jesuit missions and fewer military expeditions on the high plains. His
complaints are one reason General Sully will be called to account for his decisions, his actions during the campaign in Dakota and Montana.

Father De Smet is the most famous of many determined, du-
rable, sympathetic Jesuits who would take up residence in what
became Montana, including Father Ravalli and Father Giorda
(who was taken captive by Bull Lodge for a brief time in 1862).
Yet the tension between Catholic discipline and native customs
will cause pain and misunderstanding on both sides of this massive cultural divide, the theology of hell and damnation a strange
overlay on the piety of medicine men such as Bull Lodge. When
that faith becomes a technology for remaking Indian children
in the image of pious Christians, deformation, agony, and regret
will follow.

D'Arcy McNickle's 1936 novel *The Surrounded*, set on the
Flathead Indian reservation, provides a sophisticated, multi-
layered evaluation of the Jesuits' legacy in the region, using the
character of Father Grepilloux as a composite portrait of piety,
decency, and unintended consequences. As McNickle's narrator
observes of the legendary priest upon his death,

> His greatest sorrow was the decay of the Missions, when
> Congress, because of the pressure of certain religious

spokesmen, refused to allow funds already owing certain tribes to be used, at the request of the tribes, for the support of Mission schools. The burden had become too great. In the early years priests and nuns had got their funds by going out on annual begging tours of mining camps and settlements. Latterly that and other sources of revenue failed, and when Congress refused support the Mission schools languished....That was the missionary priest, as his own book revealed him—a man of prodigious labors, a priest of gifted insight and broad sympathy, and a pathfinder. Max Leon could think of him in all these ways. And now that the priest lay dead, he could ask himself what it signified. Blasphemous thought, but Max could not rid his mind of it. What good had been accomplished? What evil?

McNickle's later novel, *Wind from an Enemy Sky*, tells the story of boarding schools from the perspective of young Antoine, a coming-man who has returned to his people's world in the midst of crisis over the building of a dam on sacred waters. Antoine carries bitter memories of his time at the white man's school, memories he shares with his powerful grandfather Bull because he sympathizes with the anger surging in the proud leader who is deciding how to respond to the affront, the disrespect, the profanity of the dam:

> The disciplinarian at the government's school tried to be a big man. He whipped us with a leather belt. But you could cut him to pieces. When I went to bed at night with a sore backside, I made pictures in my mind. I saw you take his whip away and knock him down. It made my hurt go away. His name was Mr. Monroe, but they called him the disciplinarian.

In 1890, Granville Stuart will send three of his youngest children, Sam, Harry, and Irene, to the St. Ignatius Catholic Mission. Stuart will be in the process of distancing himself from his marriage to Awbonnie and the children of their union. Following his Shoshone wife's death in the autumn of 1888, he moves swiftly to marry a young white woman and establish a new life dedicated to respectability in the just-created state of Montana. Stuart had often contemplated leaving his mixed-race family, largely under pressure from his mother, offended by her son's connection to an Indian woman, yet he had chosen to stay until Awbonnie's passing. Without the emotional and ethical bonds of that marriage, he chooses to see his youngest children as Indians, best cared for and educated in a Catholic boarding school that should have been anathema to the long-time agnostic. Granville Stuart's choices reveal much about the Montana taking shape in the late nineteenth century.

NOVEMBER

In which the Sand Creek Massacre is told, Sweet Medicine prophesies the Cheyenne future, and Higgins, Worden, and Pattee begin building Missoula Mills.

November is the moon to knock bullberries off of their thornie
bushes, cold and frost really turns them on for the sweetness.
All animal hair is prime in November, trapping begins for
those early ancestors of ours. The eagle goes on its southern
migration. Ice covers most waters.

O N NOVEMBER 29, 700 COLORADO MILITIA ATTACK THE camp of Black Kettle, a Cheyenne chief committed to peace with the Americans, killing as many as 163, mostly women and children. The Sand Creek Massacre compels surviving Cheyenne and Araphoe to journey north to join their kin, intensifying conflict in Montana Territory.

1864: A YEAR FRESH FROM THE CENTURY OF enlightenment. A year in the cauldron of civil war. In a time of severity and struggle, Black Kettle, chief of 600 Cheyennes, led his people following buffalo along the Arkansas River of Kansas and Colorado. The trees looked barely alive, waiting on storms and flash rivers, roots like slender fingers seeking water in the deep underground and Black Kettle saw their withered form and continued on from there and brought the Cheyennes to Big

Sandy Creek in the Colorado territory. Though they had
no signed treaty, he and his people relied on good will,
camping near the white man's outpost called Fort Lyon,
where he meant to make peace and accept sanctuary....

Black Kettle raised an American flag and a white flag of
peace over his tipi.

[Col. John M.] Chivington raised a hand to quiet his men.

He sat astride a big-haunched pale horse on hardscrabble
dirt under the gray pre-dawn sky....Chivington positioned his men, along with their four howitzers, around
the Cheyenne village of Black Kettle.

"Remember boys, big and little, nits grow up to make lice.
Kill them all."

AND EARLY THAT MORNING CHIVINGTON ATTACKED THE
village, and I guess you read about that. There are some
awful stories told by the Indians. Black Bear's wife had a
big scar where she was shot, and they called her One Eye
Comes Together. She told some awful stories, killing the
children, too; she saw soldiers shooting down the little
ones. And John Smith said, when they had that investiga-
tion, your boy that was packing was hit right on the back,
and was dead by the time she got over there. And the
woman was shot in the shoulder.

This was Three Fingers, the same Three Fingers that
taught us at the school over here. His younger brother
was killed there on his mother's back; she thought he was
asleep, but when she got into some shelter with the other
women and she took him down, he was dead. I knew

this woman—she was still living when I came back from school in 1905, and she must have been about seventy or eighty maybe; she was an old woman, and Black Bear married her after Sand Creek.

BUFFALO CALF ROAD WOMAN IS A CHILD OF ELEVEN WHEN SHE flees the massacre at Sand Creek. Bereft of her beloved parents, she travels north in search of her relatives in the Yellowstone country, reaching Chief Dull Knife's camp after a month of tortuous cross-country wandering, near starvation, denied shelter and clothing. She will be among the first to arrive among the Northern Cheyenne to tell of the atrocity at Sand Creek, a story that will intensify the peoples' belief in the need to resist invasion. She will grow to be a woman warrior, reputed to be the first to strike Custer at the Battle of the Little Bighorn. Even such a triumph can never wipe out the loss on that November day in 1864.

SWEET MEDICINE, THE GREAT CHEYENNE MEDICINE MAN, prophesies his people's future:

> My grandchildren listen to me. In the future, this land
> will be changing. Strange people called earth men will
> come into this country, meaning members of the earth,
> not from above. They are hairy bodied. Their ways are
> powerful. Their buffalo are spotted and smaller than
> your buffalo. They will take possession of your land and
> you will adopt their ways. Your nation and tribal law will
> gradually vanish. You people shall learn their laws, you
> shall leave your religion. New things will come up you
> will rather have. An animal will come from the east with
> round feet and his tail nearly touches the ground; there is
> long hair on his neck; you shall ride this animal and ride
> as far as you can see in one day.

Your buffalo will disappear and you will eat the strange
buffalo. Game will be less than now. Then the time will
be when you take things from other tribes, and rather
not think of your own laws; you will consider yourselves
old when you get to be men. Boys and girls will be married too young, and your people will marry one another
within the same family. Cheyenne laws prohibit marrying
too young and marrying relatives.

All these things will be changed; be aware and watch
among your nation. There will be a baby born with teeth
and white hair. This is a sign your nation will vanish.

THEY BEGIN BUILDING THEIR SAWMILL ON RATTLESNAKE CREEK
where it enters the Hell Gate River. C.P. Higgins, Frank Worden,
and David Pattee will move the center of their commercial enterprise from the cluster of twelve buildings four miles to the
west to this location at the mouth of the renowned Hell Gate
Canyon, so named because of its history of concealing war parties lying in wait for nations returning from the buffalo ranges
east of the mountains.

The settlement called Hell Gate has flourished as a key supply
point on the Mullan Road, as many as five pack trains a day
passing through from Walla Walla to the mining towns blowing
up to the east. Higgins and Worden had brought a freight load
from the Columbia River port in 1860, determined to build a
trading center for the prospective communities in the Hell
Gate, Bitterroot, and Missouri valleys. They at first considered
establishing their post in the Bitterroot Valley, close to John
Owen's fort, but chose instead the Hell Gate Ronde, as it was
rather grandly named, a meeting point of five valleys and so an
appropriate location to trade with native peoples and migrating

Captain Christopher Power Higgins. Montana Historical Society Research Center Photograph Archives, Helena, Montana

whites. A key partner, Frank Woody, will recall of activity at Hell
Gate in 1864:

> The Kootenai mines having been discovered early in the
> spring of this year, hundreds of men flocked to them,
> passing by the village of Hell's Gate. This stampede creat-
> ed a demand for all kinds of supplies, and everything sold
> at war prices. In the spring of this year, seed wheat sold
> as high as $10.00, and potatoes at $6.00 per bushel; yeast
> powders were cheap at $1.50 per box, and coffee at $1.00
> per pound, and flour of the poorest quality sold read-
> ily at $30.00 per hundred pounds and everything else in
> proportion. In the fall of 1864, the ruling price for wheat
> was from four to five dollars per bushel....The currency
> at this time was principally gold dust. These high prices
> were caused by the immense number of people who had
> flocked to the mines of Alder and other gulches on the
> East side, and by the demand made by the settlers in the
> Gallatin, Jefferson and Madison valleys for seed grain and
> potatoes.

Higgins, an Irishman, had first come to know the region as a
member of Isaac Stevens' railroad survey team in 1853-54. He
had been present at the signing of the Council Grove Treaty in
1855, an event with cataclysmic consequences for the nations
that had claimed this place as home for hundreds of years.
Johnny Grant, whose stepsister, Julie, married Higgins, shared
this portrait of the town founder,

> He was not wealthy, but he was a good manager, and he
> invested his wife's money to good advantage. He began
> to keep a store; then he went into partnership with one
> Frank Worden. He afterwards organized a bank called the
> National Bank of Missoula, and he was president of it.

Frank Woody standing in front of old Worden and Company Store, Hell Gate, Montana. MONTANA HISTORICAL SOCIETY RESEARCH CENTER PHOTOGRAPH ARCHIVES, HELENA, MONTANA.

WORDEN OWNED A MERCANTILE BUSINESS IN WALLA WALLA
and was in a mood to take a risk on a coming country. While
Hell Gate Ronde has proven lucrative, the partners realize that
to maximize profit, to take advantage of the demand to the east
and the burgeoning farms in the five valleys converging near
their post, they must have the means to convert wheat to flour.
A gristmill will follow the sawmill. Flour riots in Virginia City
during the winter of '64-'65 caused by shortage and high prices
will confirm this intuition. Mills have become the bedrock, the
foundation of towns created by emigrants throughout the United States. When James Fergus dreamed of a frontier metropolis
in Minnesota, building a dam and mill were the inevitable starting points. John Bozeman had capitalized a mill for Bozeman
City just two months earlier.

And so Missoula Mills is born. The new town will be called
Worden for a time, but Frank will have nothing to do with that
self-aggrandizement, and so locals will settle on the name "Missoula," which means "the place of chilly waters" in Salish, no
doubt a reference to the snow-melt flow of streams such as the
Rattlesnake, Grant Creek, Pattee Creek, and the Hell Gate itself.
The name had first entered English usage in 1808 when David
Thompson, Northwest Company factor extraordinaire, records
this Salish word in his diary, though its full rendering will prove
daunting for an English tongue: *Nemissoolatakoo*. For the Salish,
this valley will remain the source of the bitterroot, a key medicine and food, harvested annually in spring and early summer.

DECEMBER

In which Judge Hosmer calls out the Vigilantes, Governor Edgerton calls the first territorial legislature into session, and Calamity Jane arrives in Montana.

December is the Moon of Winter Cold. It's also the Moon That Parts Her Hair Right Square in the Middle. This is because of the days, the shortest day and the beginning of the longer days.

The year that began with an outbreak of vigilante justice ends with an elegant but forceful challenge to extralegal remedies. The first appointed chief justice to the new territory, Hezekiah Hosmer, calls for an end to mob rule in Montana. The gathering of a grand jury in the Planters Hotel, Virginia City, on December 5 provides the occasion for his defense of formal legal proceedings. Hosmer is the very man to deliver this message, for he is a skilled lawyer who served as secretary to the House Committee on Territories that guided Montana into existence. His declared desire to be named Librarian of Congress suggests a literary-minded, refined gentleman, one inclined to respect established procedure and federal institutions. Yet one should not imagine a scholarly, detached citizen—Hosmer has the good sense to enter into a partnership with Nathaniel Langford and Samuel Hauser to establish a bank in Virginia City.

The lawyer from Ohio begins with tempered praise for the vigilantes' work:

The cause of Justice, hitherto deprived of the interven-
tion of regularly organized courts, has been temporarily
subserved by voluntary tribunals of the people partaking
more of the nature of self-defence than the comprehensive principles of the Common Law. It is no part of the
business of this court to find fault with what has been
done; but rather, in common with all good citizens, to
laud the transactions of an organization, which, in the
absence of law, assumed the delicate and responsible office of purging society of all offenders against its peace,
happiness and safety.

Hosmer takes pains to affirm Henry Plummer's execution
was warranted by the desperate lack of law and order:

The sources of official power had been monopolized by
the very class which preyed upon society. The greatest
villain of them all—with hands reeking with the blood of
numerous victims—was the principal ministerial officer
of the Territory, and had at his beck a band of wretches
who had become hardened in their bloody trade, years
before they came here to practice it.

And yet, the time has come to set aside these extraordinary measures and allow the emerging legal institutions to
do their work.

A threat of punishment courses just below the surface of Hosmer's carefully chosen words:

Much as we may approve the means of self-protection
thus employed, and the promptitude with which they
were applied, our admiration ceases, when they assert an
authority defiant of law, and usurp offices which belong
only, to Government itself. We give them all the credit
they deserve, by according them praise for what they have
accomplished; but they have fulfilled their work. To go

farther is to commit crime, and undo what has been so well done. No law-abiding citizen wishes their continuance. They should at once and forever be abandoned.... Let us then erect no more impromptu scaffolds. Let us inflict no more midnight executions.

While complex sentences were far more common in 19th-century writing than today, Hosmer's phrasing seems especially labored here. The qualifying phrases point to a tricky persuasive problem, how to sing the praises of the vigilantes while foreclosing any ethical or legal purpose for their going forward. Hosmer surely knows that two members of the inaugural grand jury, Thomas Baume and James Williams, are recognized members of the Vigilance Committee. The layered, even twisted sentences reveal a speaker aware of the tough sell to a skeptical audience. Perhaps the chief justice worries that vigilante tactics will be used for partisan purposes by Confederate sympathizers, a justifiable concern in context of the waning War of the Rebellion and the potential for retribution by the defeated. Just as importantly, Hosmer's very status and power will be stripped, trampled, erased if vigilante justice endures. One of three props for the young, weak territorial government—the executive, legislative, and judicial functions—will be removed, threatening to topple the entire structure.

Hosmer's courage in making even this carefully modulated statement of principle emerges from his son's memoir of the speech and its aftermath. This loyal witness observes that

> [n]o Legislature had met and the Organic Act, hardly more than a right to exist, made no provisions for the rule of procedure when courts should be organized. There was no civil or criminal code. . . .

Chief Justice Hosmer is creating a legal framework *ex nihilo*, from scratch, suggesting his defiance toward mob violence took more than a little daring. As if to underscore the judge's boldness, his son shares a sharp-edged response to this opening speech from one in attendance:

> We are glad the government has sent you here. We have some civil matters to attend to, but you had better let us take charge of the criminal affairs.

Threats can flow in both directions. And in fact, vigilantes would continue to string up suspected criminals through the early 1870s, often yielding stark injustice and cruelty. Granville Stuart will apply this logic on the open range in the early 1880s, leading a group notoriously called the Stuart Stranglers, who will kill at least eighteen suspected horse thieves. The elegant words of an Ohio lawyer, freshly arrived in a newborn territory, could not in and of themselves overcome the blood lust, the faith in the people's will, the tendency to hang first and ask questions later. They can, however, provide an index of courage in early Montana.

GOVERNOR SIDNEY EDGERTON, FULL OF PIQUE, CALLS THE first Montana territorial legislature to meet in Bannack, his home town, instead of the larger, more important Virginia City. His motives are not difficult to discern. His son-in-law, Wilbur Sanders, has been defeated in his quest to serve as Montana's first representative to Congress, the legislature is evenly divided between what Edgerton believes are true secessionists and faithful Republicans, and Virginia City is full of dangerous Democrats. The governor believes he has an advantage over his opponents on his home ground. His decision has exactly the opposite effect, for he marginalizes himself in the territory's early political life and helps assure years of confusion, mistrust, and ineffectiveness for Montana's government.

At the root of these governing challenges lies the odd nature of territorial politics. While the governor and other members of

First Legislative Hall in Bannack. MONTANA HISTORICAL SOCIETY RESEARCH CENTER PHOTOGRAPH ARCHIVES, HELENA, MONTANA.

the executive branch are appointed by the federal government, the legislature is chosen by local voters. If President Lincoln appoints fervent Republicans to the territory's administration, including Nathaniel Langford as Collector of Revenue, voters will create a split legislature including many ardent Democrats of both the union and secessionist persuasion. Montanans have long claimed the power of rebel thinking at their origin and ever after in various fringe tendencies within the state. In Joseph Kinsey Howard's famous summation of this view,

> Montana had become a Territory in its own right in May, 1864…but it nevertheless chose still to regard itself as back of beyond, as a remote, independent, and untouchable empire. It resented and continually obstructed, ungratefully, the federal controls which accompanied the blessings of territorial recognition; and an active and noisy section of its citizenry held that it should continue to be the last refuge of the Confederacy's unreconstructed belligerents. Montana has a legend to the effect that "the left wing of the army of Confederate General Price in Missouri never surrendered; it retreated to Montana."

Though the scale and depth of antipathy to Lincoln's administration have probably been exaggerated, the Montana election of 1864 demonstrates an even divide between the two political parties, encouraging distrust and obstruction.

Edgerton intensifies the partisan divide by insisting all members of the legislature take the Iron Clad Oath declaring full allegiance to the United States of America. One charismatic member, John H. Rogers, who had in fact served with Sterling Price in Missouri, must resign. The territory's first governor compounds the hard feelings by delivering a fiery speech to the assembled legislators attacking anyone who does not align with Republican principles:

Although we are far removed from the scene of strife which is devastating one portion of our country, we cannot be indifferent to the result of the struggle. We are a part of the great American Nation, and a part of that Nation we must ever remain. Her interest, her prosperity and glory must ever be dear to the heart of every loyal man. This unhallowed rebellion had its origin in the lust for power and the insane desire to extend and perpetuate human bondage. For years this conspiracy had been plotting, till at length, under the imbecile administration of James Buchanan it threw off all disguise and assumed the defiant attitude of treason. Beginning in crime and perfidy, it has sought to establish its power by atrocities the most inhuman and appalling, ignoring the long established rules of civilized warfare, it has prosecuted the war with a fiendish ferocity that would put to blush the most uncivilized savages.

In a mere six sentences, Edgerton bludgeons his auditors with his interpretation of the origin, prosecution, and inevitable result of the War of the Rebellion. He hammers home the point that the rebels—not Lincoln or the Republicans—caused the war on the basis of belief in extending slavery, a pertinent argument given the setting and occasion for his remarks, since it was precisely the creation of territories in the trans-Mississippi region that destabilized long-standing compromises maintaining the balance of slave and non-slave power in the federal government. James Buchanan, not the recently reelected Lincoln, must bear responsibility for the outbreak of hostilities. Not content with providing this gloss on the origins of war, Edgerton asserts that the seceshes have fought in such a manner that they exceed "savages" (no mistaking the allusion to Indian nations) in their barbarity. The governor has delivered a comprehensive shaming of the legislators sympathetic to a negotiated peace or to the Confederacy.

And what would be the results of this rhetorical offensive? A legislative session notable for establishing vague or incomplete laws that would bind the territorial government's hands. The first session will assure that the uncivil war will be perpetuated in the inefficiency and ineffectiveness of the territory. This original governing body meets in log buildings whose construction was supervised and paid for by Edgerton himself. Edgerton must put out $3,600 of his own money because the Lincoln administration has neglected to appoint a territorial secretary, the only official designated to requisition federal funds. Edgerton had nominated as secretary none other than Francis Thomson, supplier of a young William Andrews Clark, friend of the Vails and Henry Plummer, and determined lobbyist for the new territory, but the request may have been lost in the planning and execution of William Tecumseh Sherman's Georgia campaign. The territory would await the arrival in 1865 of the notorious Thomas Meagher, Irish rebel, Union Civil War leader, and appointee of the Andrew Johnson administration, to have the means to procure federal funds. In any case, Montana's first legislature takes up questions highlighted by the governor in other, less incendiary parts of his opening speech: realizing tax revenues through mining, road construction and maintenance, mail delivery, and education.

The legislature must also address relations with Indian peoples, and here Edgerton's opening speech rings an ominous theme:

> I trust that the Government will, at an early day, take steps for the extinguishment of the Indian title in this territory, in order that our lands may be brought into market.

These early settlers are thinking of the legal and financial opportunities offered up by the Homestead Act of 1862. All their
mapping and platting won't matter unless the land in the newly
made territory is transferred from Indian nations to the United
States, and so made subject to sale. Isaac Stevens, railroad plan-
ner, treaty-maker, and now martyr to the Union cause, having
died at the Battle of Chantilly in 1862, projected this very outcome, the conversion of tribal lands into property. Victor, Salish chief, will register his resistance to this process in a letter to
Governor Edgerton early in 1865.

The legislature's first order of business, however, is to resolve
that most contentious, fundamental question of all for citizens
living through the dying days of the Civil War: Who would have
the right to vote? After the dust-ups in Washington City during
passage of the Organic Act creating Montana, and given the nar-
rowly divided Council and House, it seems inevitable that suffrage would be granted to "all white male citizens of the United
States, and those who have declared their intention to become
citizens, above the age of twenty-one years," as long as individu-
als have resided in the territory twenty days. Montana Territory
will continue to pass legislation limiting the rights of African
Americans during its twenty-five-year existence.

These lawmakers then set about defining the more mundane
aspects of governance: number of counties (nine), number of
judicial districts (three), prohibition on gambling scams, provisions for managing livestock, organizing and taxing mining
properties, and, perhaps most importantly from the legislators'
perspective, assuring order and comity in administering justice
in the wide-open mining towns. And yet the legislature fails to
set a date for its next meeting, creating a legislative void for the
ensuing years. As this first governing body of "The Land of Shining Mountains" limps to its inevitable conclusion, one observer
colorfully observes,

The high comedy which has been on these boards for sixty days, closed Tuesday evening at 10 o'clock. The spectators were bored, the actors weary, the scenery dilapidated, and the footlights dim.

CALAMITY HAS ARRIVED IN MONTANA BY DECEMBER 31, 1864. A gambler, his prostitute wife, and their six children land in Nevada City after an arduous five-month journey from Iowa. When the pickings prove slim, the children, the oldest named Martha Jane, not to be confused with Mrs. Vail of Sun River Indian Farm, are forced to beg for food in Virginia City: "Three little girls, who state their names to be Canary, appeared at the door of Mr. Fergus, on Idaho street, soliciting charity," reports the *Montana Post*. The children have turned to none other than James Fergus, he of the volcanic temper tantrum in August, who serves as a caretaker of the poor in the new town. Fortunately, "Mrs. Fergus, Mrs. Castner and Mrs. Moon kindly provided them with food and some clothing." The children then return to Nevada City, "where they have existed for some time." For the parents the reporter spares little sympathy, describing them as "inhuman brutes who have deserted their poor, unfortunate children," showing a "most flagrant and wanton instance of unnatural conduct on the part of parents to their children."

Just eight years old when we see her for the first time on the streets of the boom town, Calamity Jane has already established the pattern of life that will define her existence on this earth until her death in 1903. Her parents will be dead within three years, and she will need to fend for herself and her younger siblings through guile, gumption, and guts.

Martha was born to a farmer of thirty-one years and his boisterous, sometimes outlandish wife of sixteen in Princeton, Missouri. Her parents made an odd couple, at least as described by those who remembered their years in the Missouri farm country: Her father, Robert, seems to have been a relatively sober, unassuming man, quite ineffective at the basic task of making a living, while her mother, Charlotte, so much younger than her spouse, was fond of dressing in colorful clothing and expressing her opinions in equally vivid language. There is not much doubt which parent Martha favors.

Her surname, Canary, will always seem ill-suited to the cocky, boisterous, loud-mouthed, profane, sentimental, dissembling, often drunk but never to be backed-down or cowed woman, unless one credits the story told by one of her acquaintances that she earned her surname by singing like a mule, the Rocky Mountain canary.

Her parents' motives for making the risky trek to Montana in '64 must remain a matter of speculation. Robert may have encountered legal difficulties in Missouri following his own father's death (the son seems to have borrowed $600 against his father's estate and was then unable to repay it). Martha will remember the journey as a chance to explore and hunt with boys and men in the wagon train. Once the Canarys arrived in Nevada City, hopes for wealth from mining plainly did not materialize, explaining how the self-righteous reporter for the *Post* could describe Robert as "a gambler in Nevada" and Charlotte as a "woman of the lowest grade." The parents are not granted a dignified death. Charlotte will pass away in 1866 after working as a washer woman for miners, while Robert will depart this earth a year later in Salt Lake City. Martha is next glimpsed at Fort Bridger, built by the legendary figure who has taken such a prominent role in guiding emigrants to the new territory, in '64. She will later tell a reporter,

> Wal, we lived near a post, an' them soldiers took care of me. I didn't know nothing 'bout women ner how white folks lived; all I knowed was to rustle grub an' steal rides behind the stage-coaches an' camp with the Injuns.

Thrown onto her own wits and devices by the age of eleven, Martha masters the street smarts of a Huck Finn to survive. She has to be protean, shape-shifting, playful, and harsh so that no one can see her fully, determine her strengths and weaknesses, take advantage of her softness. She is fond of telling tall tales about herself, creating a kind of mythical identity celebrated by popular fiction and newspapers. She gains her initial fame through the overheated prose of a western dime novel, and she has the good sense to exploit her notoriety by selling photographs of herself and joining (briefly and awkwardly) Buffalo Bill's Wild West Show. In reality, young Martha, often dressed as a scout or mule skinner, becomes a "camp follower" for military and railroad crews, a polite term for a prostitute. She later befriends famous men such as Wild Bill Hickok, shot down in Deadwood, though apparently they are never intimate. Much of her adulthood will consist of temporary partnerships, sometimes called marriages, and she gives birth to at least one child, a daughter named Jessie, though they do not see much of each other during Calamity's relatively short term on this earth. Her life alternates between stabs at respectability and episodes of outrageous public drunkenness. Her childhood experience on that cold December day in Virginia City hints at the demons that possessed her.

The nickname "Calamity" sticks to her early in life, aided by the melodramatic popular media, yet it becomes both a curse and a blessing. It names her poor luck, her unfortunate tendency to find herself in rotten circumstances: orphan, prostitute, alcoholic drifter, and lonely mother. But "Calamity" also tells of her willingness to go toward trouble to help people in need, to assuage their pain, such as a young man dying from smallpox, a cowboy kicked by a horse, or a woman suffering from ailments of the womb and the heart. Martha will so completely defy Victorian convention that few will know how to classify her: Angel or whore, who could say for sure? Calamity Jane never wants to

Martha Canary (Calamity Jane), 1876. PHOTOGRAPH BY CHARLES
PETERSON, COURTESY OF THE HOWARD COLLECTION, UNIVERSITY OF
WYOMING, LARAMIE, WY

be reduced to a type. That's one reason she remains a powerful presence in the region's memory.

AFTER

In which Mollie Sheehan dances on news of Lincoln's death, Victor sends a letter of concern to Governor Edgerton, and M. L. Smoker offers a final wisdom.

NEWS, ONLY A LITTLE BELATED, OF THE assassination of Abraham Lincoln came in by Pony Express. The little girls who were my particular friends and playmates were all the children of Southern parents. They had reawakened in me all the prejudices that were mine because of my Kentucky birth and because of association with my Missouri cousins. It pains me to recall what we did when we were told of Lincoln's death. The news reached Virginia City in April 1865. It was noon. We girls were in the schoolhouse eating our lunches, which we sometimes carried to school with us. The Southern girls, by far the majority, picked up their ankle-length skirts to their knees and jigged and hippity-hopped around and around the room. They cheered for the downfall of that great, good, simple man whom they had been taught to regard as the archenemy of the South. They believed him the first and last cause of any and every misfortune that had befallen their parents and driven them to seek new fortunes amid the hardships of a far western frontier.

—Mollie Sheehan upon learning of Lincoln's death

Now I address myself to you the Great Chief of the Whites of this country. Some of the big men among the white settlers in this our land, spoke to drive us away from our country. This thing vexed a great deal me, and all the other Chiefs, and all my children. I, Victor, therefore do send you the horse above mentioned to pray you to take pity on us, and to put an end to such talkings, and to stop the whites from building themselves houses in our land guaranteed to us by Treaty. We are almost given to dispondency seeing every day new houses started up, and farms taken by whites in our land.

—Victor's letter to Governor Sidney Edgerton, 1865

BIRTHRIGHT

for Carl Lithander

We talked once of driving all the remote gravel roads, writing from here and there, a little like Hugo, though neither of us had read his poems yet. Today I am wondering about those unwritten drafts. Could they have predicted the severity of this drought, would they have spoken to our own landscape, one of anger, sympathy and remorse: You, the eventual heir to your family's homestead; and me, an Indian woman who leases her land to white men made up of the same storm and grit and hunger as your grandfather. What if we had found a message in verse written from some small town?—abandon this place. Would we have listened and turned the car east or south and left behind the land our families have lived on for generations? But where could we travel and not long for the ache of the wind blowing over open land? And how long could we have held ourselves back, away from our need to feel claimed by a place we can only, with our limited tongue, call home.

—M. L. Smoker, 2005

ACKNOWLEDGMENTS

WE LIVE IN A GIFT ECONOMY. EACH OF US BENEFITS TIME AND again from the talents and grace of others, and we reply in kind. I'm never more reminded of this beautiful truth than when working on a book, for so many people step up to make it possible to complete the research, writing, editing, and publishing. Making a book is truly a communal achievement, whatever the name that appears on the title page.

Thanks, then, to the many wise guides for this project—you directed me to key sources, read drafts, answered my questions, and encouraged a querulous writer: Rosemary Agnito, Kim Anderson, Ellen Baumler, Mandy Smoker Broaddus, Robert Brown, Julie Cajune, Victor Charlo, Ellen Crain, Patty Dean, Jock and Jamie Doggett, Samantha Dwyer, Brian Egan, Devin Egan, Eve Egan, Richard Etulain, William Farr, Harry Fritz, Andrew Graybill, Kristi Hager, Kirby Lambert, Tim Lehman, Zena Beth McGlashan, David Mogen, David Moore, Lory Morrow, Jason Neal, Cherie Newman, Shann Ray, Kate Shanley, Barbara Theroux, Sally Thompson, Bill Turner, Alan Weltzien, and Bruce Wendt.

Thanks, also, to those elders and scholars who have shared vital knowledge of Montana in its pre- and early territorial days— your names are on display in the reference list and in the body of this book.

Chris Cauble at Riverbend Publishing showed faith in the project at a crucial moment in the book's evolution, assuring *Montana 1864* would see publication. I can't thank you enough for that vote of confidence.

And above all, my fondest thanks to Terry Ann Egan, who has supported me all the way in so many ways. You are my best Montana discovery.

SOURCES

*Note: All verbatim excerpts are indicated in the text
by quotation marks or block quotations.*

INTRODUCTION

11   *almost like Buffalo Bill; and, greatest publicity
     stunt*   Monaco and Seibold.

13   *this vast, worthless area*   Black, 95.

VISIONS

15   *you have now finished*   Horse Capture, 57.

18   *general condition of the Indians*   Upson, 297.

19   *Every man for his principles*   Dimsdale, 262.

20   *our magnificent state of Montana*   Granville Stuart, vol. 1,
     19-20.

21   *very old tribal world*   Cajune.

JANUARY

23   *months of the year had names*   Bullchild, 120.

23   *It is bitter chill*   information drawn from Bray, 76;
     Athearn, 100-115.

26   *Henry Plummer reclines*   Information drawn from Allen,
     225-29; Thompson, 141, 147, 148-52.

28   *useless for you to beg*   Allen, 227.

30   *send us all to hell*   Allen, 228.

30   *bright eyes and a quick mind*   Ronan, especially 39.

33 *savages, irredeemable* This section is based on Upson, 293-94.

34 *design of getting their lands* quoted in Ewers, 237.

35 *no one thing* Upson, 294.

35 *young man on the make* details drawn from Thompson, 244.

35 *no lack of opportunities* Dedman and Newell, 30.

36 *dry Jeff Davis Gulch* Dedman and Newell, 26.

36 *as rotten a human being* DeVoto, 72.

FEBRUARY

39 *Moon of the Eagle* Bullchild, 120.

39 *traveled the hard road from Idaho* Information from Langford, 89-96; and Black, 100-06.

40 *may be made to yield annualy* Black, 133.

43 *like the old farmer* Black, 124.

44 *Thompson leaves Bannack* Details extracted from Thompson 197-201.

45 *few days before starting* Thompson 198.

46 *Being with Judge Edgerton* Thompson, 200.

46 *calving-out season* Information about the Doggett family is drawn from Stout, vol. 2, 652-53; and Progressive Men, vol. 2, 1049.

MARCH

49 *Geese Arrive Moon* Bullchild, 120.

49 *Stuart urges his brother* Information gathered from Milner and O'Connor, 43-68, 81-84, 98-99; Granville Stuart, vol. 1, 118-31; vol. 2, 13-15.

50 *tenth day of October, 1857* Granville Stuart, vol. 1, 124.

53 *Young Mollie Sheehan* quoted material from Ronan, 45.

56 *drained by the "Yellowstone"* James Stuart, 149-50.

58 *Buffalo to be seen* James Stuart, 178.

59 *tireless gold-seekers* Campbell, 6.

60 *we will strike it rich* James Stuart, 186.

60 *agent in the area reported* Hoxie, 88.

61 *pushed on to Bannack City* James Stuart, 233.

62 *how many d—d fools & asses* Milner and O'Connor, 137.

62 seven of Johnny Grant's children are baptized Information about Grant's life is drawn from Meikle; for much more information about the Metis during the 1860s, see Vrooman.

62 *the great medicine man* Montana Post, December 16, 1865, 1.

64 *he is called here Johnny Grant* Purple, 84-85.

64 *The music for these dances* Granville Stuart, vol. 1, 193-94.

64 *twenty three large windows* Meikle, 89.

66 *living in heaven* Abbott, 145; information about Russell gathered from Taliaferro.

APRIL

69 *Moon of the Frogs* Bullchild, 120.

69 *Letter from his Excellency* Owen, vol. 1, 334-35. This fascinating text is the source for most of the information on Owen.

70 *like a King* Owen, vol. 1, 10.

72 *Indians will not be satisfied* Owen, vol. 2, 210.

72 *a dark political resurrection* Owen, vol. 2, 286-87.

73 *Help me to dodge* McPherson, 364.

73 *Vigilance party left* Owen, vol. 1, 299.

74 *emigrants are passing Hellgate* Owen, vol. 1, 302.

74 *Collins came out* Owen, vol. 1, 308.
77 *meat never spoils* Alter, 191. All information about
    Bridger is drawn from this lively source.
78 *Traveled 8 Miles & camped* Owen, vol. 1, 311.
78 *fine Bul Antelope* Owen, vol. 1, 313.
78 *Mr Parham & Myself* Owen, vol. 1, 313.
78 *The cattle Lost* Owen , vol. 1, 315.
79 *they greeted me* Owen, vol. 1, 317.
81 *Kootenai Culture Committee* Sally Thompson.

MAY

83 *Moon of the Green Grass* Bullchild, 120.
83 *hopes are blasted* Information drawn from Upson, 294-
    95, 298-99; Thompson, 33-80, 138-43; Allen, 62-69, 95-
    100, 153-54; Harkness, 351, 356; Mather and Boswell,
    9-73.
102 *Shortly after arriving at Bannack* Plassman, 337.
106 *fore part of the month of January* Upson, 298.
107 *make a civilized place* Postscript: Neither Little Dog nor
     the Sun River Indian Farm survive long after the Vails'
     departure from Montana. Little Dog will be murdered by
     his own people in 1866, likely because of his willingness
     to accommodate the white settlers; in that same year,
     Piegan warriors attack and burn down the farm buildings,
     making the farm symbolic of a failed experiment in
     converting the Blackfeet nations to agrarian life.
108 *Indians are removing the Cache* Owen, vol. 1, 129.
109 *Victor faced probably the most difficult problem* Biggart
     and Woodcock, 74.
110 *provided that the Bitter Root Valley* Biggart and
     Woodcock, 15.

110   *Lincoln stands with pen*   Information drawn from Spence, 4-15.

112   *Dosheimer kept tavern*   Plassman, 338.

112   *There are some Negroes*   Allen, 287.

JUNE

115   *Moon of Hatching*   Bullchild, 120.

115   *expenses toil & privations*   Voorhees, 26. All further quotations in this section, as well as details of his travels, are drawn from Voorhees' journal.

116   *we numbered 124 wagons*   37.

118   *in camp near 3 miles*   49.

119   *gold on [the] head waters*   50-51.

120   *came along in a buggy*   54-55.

121   *& here the horsemen*   52.

122   *just below an Indian camp*   56.

123   *first house since leaving the Platt*   60.

123   *"& now we are in Virginia*   61.

124   *Towards morning, before the light*   Long, 28-30.

JULY

127   *Moon of Ripe Berries*   Bullchild, 121.

127   *Sully is distracted, irritable*   Information on Sully's 1864 campaign is drawn from Athearn, 135-43; Drury and Clavin, 172-73; Larson, 44-49; Sully, 180-209; and Scott and Kempcke. Information on Sully's attempt to forestall the Marias Massacre is drawn from Graybill, 107-09.

127   *emigrant wagons and ox-teams*   Athearn, 134.

131   *under everybody's feet*   Larson, 47.

134   *Fourth of July in Benton*   Overholser, 379.

136 *way to fix that sort* Overholser, 279

136 *dozen uncouth houses* Sunder, 260-61.

136 *we…say to strangers* Overholser, 49.

138 *"superior race" transformed* Dew, 15.

138 *the last of her race* Dew, 30.

140 *streets of a rough-and-tumble town* For the best treatment of the Civil War's impact on Montana, see Robison.

140 *minister with strong Southern sympathies* Information about L.B. Stateler is drawn from Edwin Stanley, Safford, and Johnson.

141 *Hot Spring District* Safford, 6.

143 *a party of seven or eight* Reginald Stanley, 8.

AUGUST

147 *summer holy encampment* Bullchild, 121.

147 *outnumbered Apsáalooke* Crow Tribal History Project, Timeline.

147 *Lacota and Cheyenne came together* Linderman, Pretty-shield, 43-44.

148 *We swung our lines around* Linderman, Plenty-coups, 257-61.

150 *daylight spread over the Pryor Creek valley* Bray, 67-69. The Battle of Arrow Creek, also called the Battle of the Defended Tents by the Sioux, a legendary confrontation between the combined forces of the Sioux, Cheyenne and Arapaho against the Crows, has been variously dated as occurring in 1862, 1863 or 1864. I use the year 1864 since this is the date provided by the Crow tribe's official history.

151 *Mrs. Fergus I have not had an opportunity* Peavy and
     Smith, 194-95. All information about Pamelia and James
     Fergus is gathered from this readable, well-researched
     book

153 *Minnesota got rid* Peavy and Smith, 120.

154 *not a man of them was hung* Peavy and Smith, 139.

154 *General Pope has been sent* Peavy and Smith, 127.

157 *next time I cross the planes* Peavy and Smith, 185.

157 *Blanchard observes with evident disgust* McDermott, 12.

158 *On the 23rd of August, Gad Upson* Upson, 296.

159 *I do not anticipate any trouble* Upson, 296.

159 *Bull Lodge, a revered medicine man* With the exception
     of the passage from Fowler, all information about Bull
     Lodge's visions and life is drawn from Horse Capture.

161 *people all around you* Horse Capture, 53.

162 *he would "distribute robes* Fowler, 37.

162 *living over my father's awful death* Horse Capture, 99.

163 *Settlers of Upper East Gallatin* Burlingame, 21.

164 *who exactly is this* Information about Bozeman is drawn
     from Burlingame, Black, and Johnson.

164 *spoke eloquently of its many advantages* Burlingame, 22.

166 *Tell Cathrine I would like* Burlingame, 26.

169 *only extensive game country* Kirkpatrick, 6

170 *Bozeman's restless activity* Burlingame, 13.

172 *Captain Bozeman being authorized* Burlingame, 34.

172 *made a great amount of money* Burlingame, 28.

172 *no use for money* Burlingame, 24.

174 *Frog Creek Circle* Birthright, 27.

SEPTEMBER

175   *long time rain comes* Bullchild, 121.

175   *Malcolm Clarke still carries* Information is taken from
      Clarke, 255-59; Black, 143-46, 170-71; Graybill, 8-9, 47-
      53, 81, 89-93, 262, n. 56; Ewers, 74-99. Clarke is murdered
      by Owl Child in 1869, possibly in revenge for rape of
      Owl Child's wife. That incident would lead to the Marias
      Massacre of January 23, 1870. Coth-co-co-na would
      never recover emotionally from her husband's murder at
      a kinsman's hands.

184   *I look upon this tribe* Upson, 300.

184   *condition of the Indians in this agency* Upson, 300.

185   *The Man from Washington* Welch, 31.

OCTOBER

187   *Geese Go South* Bullchild, 121.

188   *Frank Beck, who arrives* Information about Frank Beck is
      drawn from McGlashan, 187-92.

188   *four German gold prospectors* German Gulch Website;
      information in this section is gathered from this well-
      researched site, Malone's *Battle for Butte*, and Merritt's
      " 'The Coming Man from Canton.' " The groundbreaking
      study of the Chinese role in early Montana is Swartout.

189   *Chinese immigrants first came* Merritt, 307-308.

190   *Union ratification meeting* Montana Post, October 22,
      1864, 1.

193   *the nation of the Flatheads* Carriker, 49.

193   *One cannot help being anxious* De Smet, 118.

194   *innumerable herds of buffalo* De Smet, 243.

196   *the General's declaration* De Smet, 86.

197   *decay of the Missions* McNickle, *The Surrounded*, 138.

197 *tried to be a big man* McNickle, *Wind from an Enemy Sky*, 9. For a fuller treatment of the boarding school movement and its consequences, see Adams, especially 5-27.

NOVEMBER

199 to knock bullberries off Bullchild, 121.

199 *century of Enlightenment* Ray, 25-28.

200 *Chivington attacked the village* Stands in Timber, 114.

201 *a child of eleven* Information drawn from Agnito and Agnito, 12-13; Buffalo Calf Road Woman's presence at the Sand Creek Massacre is speculative, based on her status as a Southern Cheyenne girl of the right age to have experienced the atrocity.

201 *this land will be changing* Stands in Timber, 311-12.

202 *sawmill on Rattlesnake Creek* Information about Missoula is drawn from Koelbel and Woody.

204 *Kootenai mines having been discovered* Woody, 102.

204 *He was not wealthy* Meikle, 84.

DECEMBER

207 *Moon of Winter Cold* Bullchild, 121.

208 *cause of Justice, hitherto deprived* Montana Post, December 10, 1864, 1. All further quotations from Hezekiah Hosmer's speech are drawn from this source.

209 *[n]o Legislature had met* Hosmer, 291.

210 *glad the Government has sent* Hosmer, 292.

212 *Territory in its own right* Howard, 38.

213 *the scene of strife* Edgerton, 347.

215 *the extinguishment* Edgerton, 344.

215 *all white male citizens* Spence, 26-27. This source is the
    key to information for the current section.

216 *high comedy* Spence, 29.

216 *Three little girls* and other quotations in this
    paragraph *Montana Post*, December 31, 1864, 2. All
    other information about Calamity Jane is drawn from
    McLaird, the closest to a definitive biography we are likely
    to have.

218 *them soldiers took care of me* McLaird, 153.

AFTER

221 *News, only a little belated* Ronan, 47-48.

222 *Some of the big men* Victor, 56.

223 *driving all the remote gravel roads* Smoker, 46.

REFERENCES

Abbott, E. C. ("Teddy Blue"), and Helena Huntington Smith. *We Pointed Them North: Recollections of a Cowpuncher*. Ca. 1939. Reprint Norman: University of Oklahoma Press, 1955.

Adams, David Wallace. *Education for Extinction: American Indians and the Boarding School Experience, 1875-1928*. Lawrence: University Press of Kansas, 1995.

Agnito, Joseph and Rosemary. *Buffalo Calf Road Woman: The Story of a Warrior of the Little Bighorn*. Helena: TwoDot, 2005.

Allen, Frederick. *A Decent, Orderly Lynching: The Montana Vigilantes*. Norman: University of Oklahoma Press, 2004.

Alter, J. Cecil. *Jim Bridger*. Norman: University of Oklahoma Press, 1961.

Athearn, Robert G. *Forts of the Upper Missouri*. Lincoln: University of Nebraska Press, 1967.

Bigart, Robert, and Clarence Woodcock. *In the Name of the Salish & Kootenai Nation: The 1855 Hell Gate Treaty and the Origin of the Flathead Indian Reservation*. Pablo: Salish Kootenai Press, 1996.

Birthright: Born to Poetry—A Collection of Montana Indian Poetry. Compiled by Dorothea M. Susag. Helena: Montana Office of Public Instruction, 2012.

Black, George. *Empire of Shadows: The Epic Story of Yellowstone*. New York: St. Martin's, 2012.

Bray, Kingsley M. *Crazy Horse: A Lakota Life*. Norman: University of Oklahoma Press, 2006.

Bullchild, Percy. *The Sun Came Down*. San Francisco: Harper and Row, 1985.

Burlingame, Merrill G. *John M. Bozeman: Montana Trailmaker*. Bozeman: Museum of the Rockies, 1983.

Cajune, Julie. Montana Tribes Digital Archives: http:// montanatribes.org/digital_archives/meet_the_speakers/ JCa.html Accessed 28 November 2013.

Campbell, J. L. Idaho: *Six Months in the New Gold Diggings: The Emigrant's Guide Overland*. Chicago: John L. Walsh, 1864.

Carriker, Robert C. *Father Peter John De Smet: Jesuit in the West*. Norman: University of Oklahoma Press, 1995.

Clarke, Helen P. "A Sketch of Malcolm Clarke, A Corporate Member of the Historical Society of Montana." *Contributions to the Historical Society of Montana*. Vol. 2. Helena: State Publishing Company, 1896. 255-68.

Crow Tribal History Project. http://lib.lbhc.edu/index. php?q=node/17/ Accessed 28 November 2013.

Dedman, Bill, and Paul Clark Newell, Jr. *Empty Mansions: The Mysterious Life of Huguette Clark and the Spending of a Great American Fortune*. New York: Ballantine, 2013.

De Smet, Pierre-Jean. *Life, Letters and Travels of Father Pierre-Jean DeSmet, S. J., 1801-1873*, Volume 1. Ed. Hiram Martin Chittendon and Alfred Talbot Richardson. New York: Francis P. Harper, 1905.

DeVoto, Bernard. *Mark Twain in Eruption*. New York: Harper, 1940.

Dew, Charles B. *Apostles of Disunion: Southern Secessionist Commissioners and the Causes of the Civil War*. Charlottesville: University of Virginia Press, 2001.

Dimsdale, Thomas J. *The Vigilantes of Montana, Being a Correct and Impartial Narrative of the Chase, Trial, Capture, and Execution of Henry Plummer's Notorious Road Agent Band.* Ca. 1865. Reprint: Norman: University of Oklahoma Press, 1953.

Drury, Bob, and Tom Clavin. *The Heart of Everything That Is: The Untold Story of Red Cloud, An American Legend.* New York: Simon and Schuster, 2013.

Edgerton, Sidney E. "Governor Edgerton's First Message to the First Legislative Assembly in the Territory of Montana." *Contributions to the Montana Historical Society*, Vol. 3. Helena: State Publishing Company, 1900. 341-48.

Ewers, John C. *The Blackfeet: Raiders on the Northwestern Plains.* Norman: University of Oklahoma Press, 1958.

Fowler, Loretta. *Shared Symbols, Contested Meanings: Gros Ventre Culture and History, 1778-1984.* Ithaca: Cornell University Press, 1987.

German Gulch Website. http://www.cas.umt.edu/germangulch//default.cfm Accessed 16 February 2014.

Graybill, Andrew R. *The Red and the White: A Family Saga of the American West.* New York: Liveright, 2013.

Harkness, James. "Diary of James Harkness, of the firm La Barge, Harkness, and Company." *Contributions to the Historical Society of Montana*, Vol. 2. Helena: State Publishing Company, 1896. 343-61.

Horse Capture, George P., ed. *The Seven Visions of Bull Lodge, as told by his daughter, Garter Snake. Gathered by Fred B. Gone.* Lincoln: University of Nebraska Press, 1980.

Hosmer, J. H. "Biographical Sketch of Hezekiah L. Hosmer, First Chief Justice of the Territory of Montana." *Contributions to the Historical Society of Montana.* Vol. 3. Helena: State Publishing Company, 1900. 288-99

Howard, Joseph Kinsey. *Montana: High, Wide, and Handsome.* New Haven: Yale University Press, 1943.

Hoxie, Frederick E. *Parading through History: The Making of the Crow Nation in America 1805-1935*. New York: Cambridge University Press, 1995.

Johnson, Dorothy M. *The Bloody Bozeman: The Perilous Trail to Montana's Gold*. New York: McGraw-Hill, 1971.

Koelbel, Leonora. *Missoula the Way It Was: A Portrait of an Early Western Town*. Missoula: Gateway, 1972.

Kirkpatrick, James. *Historical Reprints: A Reminiscence of John Bozeman*. Ed. Paul C. Phillips. Missoula: State University of Montana, 1927.

Langford, Nathaniel Pitt. *Vigilante Days and Ways: The Pioneers of the Rockies, the Makers and Making of Montana, Idaho, Oregon, Washington, and Wyoming*. Missoula: Montana State University Press, 1957.

Larson, Robert W. *Gall: Lakota War Chief*. Norman: University of Oklahoma Press, 2007.

Linderman, Frank B. *Plenty-coups: Chief of the Crows*. Ca. 1930. Reprint Lincoln: University of Nebraska Press, 1962.

——. *Pretty-shield: Medicine Woman of the Crows*. Ca. 1932. Reprint Lincoln: University of Nebraska Press, 1972.

Long, James L. *Land of Nakoda: The Story of the Assiniboine Indians: From the Tales of the Old Ones Told to First Boy (James L. Long)*. Ca. 1942. Reprint Helena: Riverbend Publishing, 2004.

McDermott, John D. *Red Cloud's War: The Bozeman Trail, 1866-1868*. Norman: Arthur H. Clark, 2010.

McGlashan, Zena Beth. *Buried in Butte*. Butte: Wordz & Ink Publishing, 2010.

McLaird, James D. *Calamity Jane: The Woman and the Legend*. Norman: University of Oklahoma Press, 2005.

McNickle, D'Arcy. *The Surrounded*. Ca. 1936. Rpt. Albuquerque: University of New Mexico Press, 1978.

——. *Wind from an Enemy Sky*. Ca. 1978. Reprint Albuquerque: University of New Mexico Press, 1988.

McPherson, James. *Battle Cry of Freedom: The Civil War Era*. New York: Oxford University Press, 1988.

Malone, Michael P. *The Battle for Butte: Mining and Politics on the Northern Frontier, 1864-1906*. Seattle: University of Washington Press, 1981.

——, Richard B. Roeder, and William L. Lang. *Montana: A History of Two Centuries*. Revised edition. Seattle: University of Washington Press, 1991.

Mather, R. E., and F. E. Boswell. *Hanging the Sheriff: A Biography of Henry Plummer*. Salt Lake City: University of Utah Press, 1987.

Meikle, Lyndel, ed. *Very Close to Trouble: The Johnny Grant Memoir*. Pullman: Washington State University Press, 1996.

Merritt, Christopher William. "'The Coming Man from Canton': Chinese Experience in Montana (1862-1943)." Dissertation, University of Montana, 2010.

Milner, Clyde A., II, and Carol A. O'Connor. *As Big as the West: The Pioneer Life of Granville Stuart*. New York: Oxford University Press, 2009.

Monaco, Paul and Dennis Seibold. *Odyssey: The Montana Centennial Train, 1964-65*. Film produced by Montana State University Film and Media Department, 1989.

Montana Post. Volumes 1 and 2, September, 1864-December, 1865. Virginia City.

Overholser, Joel. *Fort Benton: World's Innermost Post*. Helena: Falcon Press, 1987.

Owen, John. *The Journals and Letters of Major John Owen, Pioneer of the Northwest, 1850-1871.* Ed. Paul C. Phillips and Seymour Dunbar. New York: E. Eberstadt, 1927.

Peavy, Linda, and Ursula Smith. *The Gold Rush Widows of Little Falls: A Story Drawn from the Letters of Pamelia and James Fergus.* St. Paul: Minnesota Historical Society Press, 1984.

Plassman, Martha Edgerton. "Biographical Sketch of Hon. Sidney Edgerton, First Territorial Governor." Contributions to the Montana Historical Society. Vol. 3. Helena: State Publishing Company, 1900. 331-40

Progressive Men of the State of Montana. Chicago: A. W. Bowen, 1901?

Purple, Edwin Ruthven. *Perilous Passage: A Narrative of the Montana Gold Rush, 1862-63.* Helena: Montana Historical Society Press, 1995.

Ray, Shann. "Black Kettle: A Triptych." Fugue. Winter/Spring, 2012: 25-35.

Robison, Ken. *Montana Territory and the Civil War: A Frontier Forged on the Battlefield.* Charleston: The History Press, 2013.

Ronan, Mary. *Girl from the Gulches: The Story of Mary Ronan. As told to Margaret Ronan.* Ed. Ellen Baumler. Helena: Montana Historical Society Press, 2003.

Safford, Jeffrey J. *The Mechanics of Optimism: Mining Companies, Technology, and the Hot Springs Gold Rush, Montana Territory, 1864-1868.* Boulder: University of Colorado Press, 2004.

Scott, Kim Allen, and Ken Kempcke. "A Journey to the Heart of Darkness: John W. Wright and the War against the Sioux, 1863-65." Montana The Magazine of Western History, 50: 4 (Winter 2000): 2-17.

Smoker, M. L. *Another Attempt at Rescue*. Brooklyn: Hanging
    Loose Press, 2005.

Spence, Clark C. *Territorial Politics and Government in
    Montana, 1864-89*. Urbana: University of Illinois Press,
    1975.

Stands in Timber, John, and Margot Liberty. *A Cheyenne Voice:
    The Complete John Stands in Timber Interviews*. Norman:
    University of Oklahoma Press, 2013.

Stanley, Edwin James. *Life of L.B. Stateler: A Story of Life on the
    Old Frontier*. Nashville: Smith and Lamar, 1916.

Stanley, Reginald. "Prologue." *From the Quarries of Last Chance
    Gulch: A "News-History" of Helena and Its Masonic
    Lodges*. William C. Campbell, ed. Helena: Montana
    Record Publishing Company, 1951. 3-10.

Stout, Tom, ed. *Montana: Its Story and Biography: A History of
    Aboriginal and Territorial Montana and Thirty Years of
    Statehood*. Chicago: American Historical Society, 1921.

Stuart, Granville. *Forty Years on the Frontier*. Ed. Paul C.
    Phillips. Cleveland: Arthur H. Clark Company, 1925.

Stuart, James. "The Yellowstone Expedition of 1863."
    Contributions to the Historical Society of Montana. Vol.
    1. Helena: Rocky Mountain Publishing Company, 1876.
    149-233.

Sully, Langdon. *No Tears for the General: The Life of Alfred
    Sully, 1821-1879*. Palo Alto: American West Publishing,
    1974.

Sunder, John E. *The Fur Trade on the Upper Missouri, 1840-
    1865*. Norman: University of Oklahoma Press, 1965.

Swartout, Robert R., Jr. "From Kwangtung to the Big Sky: The
    Chinese Experience in Frontier Montana." Montana The
    Magazine of Western History, 38: 1 (Winter 1988): 42-53.

Taliaferro, John. *Charles M. Russell: The Life and Legend of America's Cowboy Artist*. Boston: Little, Brown, 1996.

Thompson, Francis M. *A Tenderfoot in Montana: Reminiscences of the Gold Rush, the Vigilantes, and the Birth of Montana Territory*. Ed. Kenneth N. Owens. Helena: Montana Historical Society Press, 2004.

Thompson, Sally, compiler and editor, with the Kootenai Culture Committee and Pikkuni Traditional Association. *People Before the Park: Kootenai and Blackfeet in the Century before Glacier National Park*. Forthcoming from Montana Historical Society Press, 2014.

Upson, Gad E. "Report of Montana Superintendent, Blackfoot Agency." Annual report of the commissioner of Indian affairs, for the year 1864. Pp.293-303. Accessed at http://digital.library.wisc.edu/1711.dl/History.AnnRep64

Victor. From Sidney Edgerton Family Papers, 1859–1884. Manuscript Collection 26 [box 1 folder 8a]. Montana Historical Society Research Center. Archives. Excerpted in *Not In Precious Metals Alone: A Manuscript History of Montana*. Helena: Montana Historical Society Press, 1976: 56–57.

Voorhees, Abram H. "Diary." In *Bound for Montana: Diaries from the Bozeman Trail*. Ed. Susan Badger Doyle. Helena: Montana Historical Society Press, 2004. Pp. 21-62.

Vrooman, Nicholas C. P. *"The Whole Country was...'One Robe'": The Little Shell Tribe's America*. Helena: Little Shell Tribe of Chippewa Indians of Montana and Drumlummon Institute, 2012.

Welch, James. *Riding the Earthboy 40*. Ca. 1971. New York: Penguin, 2004.

Woody, Judge F. H. "A Sketch of the Early History of Western Montana. (Written in 1876 and 1877.)" Contributions to

the Historical Society of Montana. Vol. 2: 88-106. Helena:
State Publishing Company, 1896.

PERMISSIONS

Quotations used as chapter epigraphs are from *The Sun Came Down* by Percy
Bullchild. Copyright © 1985 Percy Bullchild. Reprinted by permission
of HarperCollins Publishers.

Excerpts from *Plenty-Coups, Chief of the Crows* by Frank B. Linderman.
Copyright 1930 by Frank B. Linderman. Copyright © renewed 1957 by
Norma Linderman Waller, Verne Linderman and Wilda Linderman.
Reprinted by permission of HarperCollins Publishers.

Excerpt from *The Gold Rush Widows of Little Falls: A Story Drawn from
the Letters of Pamelia and James Fergus* by Linda Peavy and Ursula
Smith. Copyright © 1984. Reprinted by permission of the Minnesota
Historical Society Press.

Excerpt from *Crazy Horse: A Lakota Life,* by Kingsley M. Bray. Copyright
2006 by the University of Oklahoma Press. Reprinted by permission.
All rights reserved.

Excerpt from *Land of Nakoda: The Story of the Assiniboine Indians: From
the Tales of the Old Ones Told to First Boy (James L. Long),* by James
L. Long. Copyright 1942. Reprinted by permission of Riverbend
Publishing.

Excerpt from *People Before the Park: Kootenai and Blackfeet in the Century
Before Glacier National Park*, by Sally Thompson, compiler and
editor, with the Kootenai Culture Committee and Pikkuni Traditional
Association. Forthcoming. Reprinted by permission of Montana
Historical Society Press.

"The Man from Washington," from *Riding The Earthboy 40* by James Welch,
copyright © 1971, 1976, 1990 by James Welch. Used by permission of
Penguin, a division of Penguin Group (USA) LLC.

"Birthright," from *Another Attempt at Rescue*, by M. L. Smoker, copyright
2005. Reprinted by permission of Hanging Loose Press.

"Frog Creek Circle," by Victor Charlo, from *Birthright: Born to Poetry—A
Collection of Montana Indian Poetry*, compiled by Dorothea M. Susag.
Copyright 2012. Reprinted by permission of Victor Charlo.

INDEX

Arapho Indians 150–151, 199
Assiniboine Indians 123–124
Bannack 97
Bannock Indians 32, 50, 56, 143, 154
Beck, J.F. "Frank" 188
Benton City. *See* Fort Benton
Bitterroot valley 107–108
Black Bear (Southern Cheyenne) 200
Blackfeet Indians 55, 62, 83, 85, 108, 181; and Sun River Indian Ranch 104
Blackfeet Treaty of 1855 34, 83
Blanchard, Jonathan 157
Blood Indians 183
Blood tribe of Blackfeet 66
Bozeman; creation 163
Bozeman, John 115, 116, 163–173
Bozeman Trail; travel on 115–224
Bridger, Jim 74–78, 120, 170–171
Brown, George 28
Brown, John 139
Buchanan, James 213
Buffalo Calf Road Woman 201
Bull Lodge (Gros Ventre) 17, 159–163, 196
Butte; 1864 gold rush 187–189; Chinese in 189–190
Cajune, Julie 21
Calamity Jane 216–224
Calf Shirt, The (Piegan) 176
Canary, Charlotte 217
Canary, Martha Jane. *See* Calamity Jane
Canary, Robert 217
Charlo (Salish) 110

Charlo, Victor 174
Cheyenne Indians (Northern) 150, 171, 171–172; and Bozeman Trail 169–170
Cheyenne Indians (Southern) 199–201
Chinese community; in Butte 189–190
Civil War; effects on Montana Territory 137–140, 210–215
Clarke, Akseniski 176
Clarke, Coth-co-co-na 175–183
Clarke, Horace 178, 183
Clarke, Malcolm 105, 144, 175–183
Clarke, Nellie 178, 182–183
Clark, William Andrews 35–37
Cleveland, Jack 92–93, 95, 98
Clubfoot George 33
Confederate Gulch 144–145
Council Grove Treaty 108–110, 204
Cover, Thomas 171, 172–173
Cow Island 137, 158
Crazy Horse (Sioux) 150–151
Crow Indians 55, 147–150
Dance, W.B. 170
Davies, W.J. 172
De Smet, Pierre-Jean 109, 193–196
Diamond City 145
Dimsdale, Thomas 33, 190
Doggett, Jefferson Davis 47
Edgerton, Sidney 39–40, 192, 210–214
Fergus, James 151–158
Fergus, Pamelia 151–158, 216
Flathead Indians 50, 56
Fort Benton 34, 88, 134–136, 134–137

Fort Laramie Treaty of 1851 194
Gallagher, Jack 32–33, 33
Gallatin City 164
German Gulch 189
Grant, John T. "Johnny" 62–65, 204
Gros Ventre Indians 34–35, 83,
    158–166, 181
Harris, Thomas W. 73
Hauser, Samuel 60, 170
He Dog (Sioux) 151
Helena 141–144
Helm, Boone 19
Higgins, C.P. 202–204
Higgins, Julie 204
Hosmer, Hezekiah 190, 207–210
Hurlbut, Allen 115–123
Indian boarding schools 192–193,
    197–198
Jacobs, Emma 167–168
Jacobs, John 167–168
Jocko valley 108
Kootenai Indians 79–81, 108
Lame Bull's Treaty 181
Langford, Nathaniel 39–44, 170,
    212
Lincoln, Abraham 110, 112, 190,
    192, 212
Little Dog (Piegan) 88–89, 90–91,
    107, 183
McAdow, P.W. 171
Mackenzie, Owen 179
McNickle, D'Arcy 196–197
Miniconjous Indians 150
Missoula; Hell Gate settlement
    202–206; naming 206
Missouri and Rocky Mountain
    Wagon Road and Telegraph
    Company 170
Montana Territory; creation 39–44,
    100, 110, 112–114; first legisla-
    ture 210–214
Mullan Road 143

National Bank of Missoula 204
Nez Perce Indians 50–51, 108, 143,
    150
One Eye Comes Together (Southern
    Cheyenne) 200
Owen, John 69–75, 171
Owen, Nancy 70
Owl Child, Pete 176, 178–179, 182
Pattee, David 202
Pend d'Oreilles Indians 108
Piegan Indians 34–35, 143; and
    Malcolm Clarke 175–183
Plenty Coups 148–150
Plummer, Electa Bryan 28–29, 83,
    85, 88, 93–99
Plummer, Henry 26, 30, 106–107;
    and Electa Bryan 92–98; and Vail
    family 98–104
Pretty Shield (Crow) 146–148
Ray, Ned 28, 30
Reed, Henry 83, 87, 89–90, 95–96
Roman Catholic church 192–198
Ronan, Mary. See Sheehan, Mollie
Russell, Charles Marion "Charlie"
    66–67
St. Ignatius Mission 192
Salish Indians 108–110, 143,
    193–194
Sand Creek Massacre (Colorado)
    199–201
Sanders, Wilbur F. 26, 190,
    191–193, 210
Sheehan, James 30–33
Sheehan, Mollie 30, 221
Shoshone Indians 50, 108, 143
Sioux Indians 55, 87
Sioux Indians (Hunkpapa) 23–26,
    127–134
Sioux Indians (Lakota) 150–151
Sioux Indians (Oglala) 150
Sisters of Providence 192
Sitting Bull (Sioux) 128–129

Smith, John; on Sand Creek Mas-
    sacre 200
Smoker, M.L. 223
Stanley, Reginald "Bob" 142
Stateler, Learner B. 140–141
Stevens, Isaac 108–110
Stevensville 70
Stinson, Buck 28, 30
Stuart, Awbonnie Tootanka 53, 54,
    198
Stuart, Ellen Lavatta 55
Stuart, Granville 20, 49–62, 64–65,
    99, 198
Stuart, Harry 198
Stuart, Irene 198
Stuart, James 49–62, 168
Stuart, Sam 198
Stuart Stranglers 210
Sully, Alfred 126–134, 194
Sun River Indian Farm 83–84,
    89–93, 97, 105–106
Swan's-head (Crow) 150
Sweet Medicine (Cheyenne) 201
Swift, Joseph 29, 89, 90, 92, 100,
    106

Thompson, Francis 44–46, 84, 89,
    90, 95, 96, 100
Three Fingers (Southern Cheyenne)
    200–201
Townsend, A.A. 171
Upson, Gad 18, 33–35, 104–105,
    158–159, 183–184
Vail, James 83–96
Vail, Martha Jane 26, 83
Victor (Salish) 107–111, 221–222
Vigilantes/Vigilance Committee
    26–29, 29, 73
Voorhees, Abram 115–123
Welch, James 185
White Clay People. See Gros Ventre
    Indians
Woody, Frank 204, 205
Worden, Frank 202–224
Word, Samuel 170
Yeager, Red 28
Young Man Afraid of His Horse
    (Sioux) 151

ABOUT THE AUTHOR

Ken Egan Jr. is the author of *Hope and Dread in Montana Literature* and *The Riven Home: Narrative Rivalry in the American Renaissance,* as well as many articles on western American literature. He co-edited *Writers Under the Rims: A Yellowstone County Anthology.* After completing his Ph.D. in American literature at the University of Wisconsin-Madison, he taught college literature and writing for 25 years. He currently serves as executive director of Humanities Montana, which provides programs and grants on history, literature, Native American Studies, and more all over the state of Montana.